F-86 Sabre Aces of the 4th Fighter Wing

SERIES EDITOR: TONY HOLMES

OSPREY AIRCRAFT OF THE ACES • 72

F-86 Sabre Aces of the 4th Fighter Wing

Warren Thompson

OSPREY
PUBLISHING

First published in Great Britain in 2006 by Osprey Publishing,
PO Box 883, Oxford, OX1 9PL, UK
PO Box 3985, New York, NY 10185-3985, USA
Email: info@ospreypublishing.com

Osprey Publishing is part of the Osprey Group.

Transferred to digital print on demand 2013

First published 2006
2nd impression 2009

Printed and bound by
Cadmus Communications, USA.

A CIP catalogue record for this book is available from the
British Library

ISBN: 978 1 84176 996 7
PDF ISBN: 978 1 4728 0252 1
ePub ISBN: 978 1 4728 0212 5

Edited by Tony Holmes
Page design by Tony Truscott
Cover Artwork by Mark Postlethwaite
Aircraft Profiles and Line Artwork by Mark Styling
Index by Alan Thatcher
Originated by PPS Grasmere, Leeds, UK

The Woodland Trust

Osprey Publishing are supporting the Woodland Trust, the
UK's leading woodland conservation charity, by funding the
dedication of trees.

www.ospreypublishing.com

Editor's note

To make this best-selling series as authoritative as possible, the
Editor would be interested in hearing from any individual who
may have relevant photographs, documentation or first-hand
experiences relating to the world's elite pilots, and their aircraft,
of the various theatres of war. Any material used will be
credited to its original source. Please write to Tony Holmes via
e-mail at:
tony.holmes@osprey-jets.freeserve.co.uk

Front cover

On the afternoon of 7 June 1953, future ten-kill ace Capt
Ralph S Parr encountered enemy MiG-15s for the very first
time whilst at the controls of an F-86F. He was no combat
novice, however, having already seen action in World War 2
and during a previous tour in Korea. Parr and his three
squadronmates from the 4th FW's 335th FS were searching
for MiG-15s, and the future ace soon spotted movement
low over the Yalu River. Diving down from 41,000 ft, he
quickly closed on his foe. However, Parr's MiG was then
joined by a further 15 communist jets! It was too late to
back off, so the Sabre pilot pressed home his attack single-
handedly. He subsequently recalled;

'After slowly overshooting, I watched the MiG leader
reverse until we were literally canopy-to-canopy in a rolling
scissors, with each of us looking into the other's cockpit. I
waited for an opportunity, and it came when the MiG pilot
made a slight change. With a little forward stick and some
rudder, I slid in behind him so close that I thought I would
hit him with the nose of my Sabre. I backed off just a bit
and was still at point blank range, which was about ten feet.
We were still right down on the deck! I could not miss, but
each time I fired, my aircraft would stall out due to the
extremely tight turn and the vibration of the guns. My only
option was to work my way through the MiG's jet wash and
into position again.

'By the time I had fired my fourth or fifth burst, my F-86
was soaked with MiG fuel. My next burst resulted in flames
streaming from the MiG back around both sides of my
aircraft and over the canopy. At that moment the MiG's
engine quit, and I shot past it just as it nosed right into the
ground and exploded. But the mission was far from over at
this point. Another MiG was closing on me from the left,
and an immediate overshoot allowed me to reverse and,
firing a long burst straight ahead, the tracers walked right
through the MiG before it could get out of range.'
Now there were five MiGs trying to cut inside, and Parr had
to pull a tight left turn to keep them at bay, but he was
being hosed down with cannon fire from all five. All of this
was playing out at almost tree-top level. He was firing at
anything that popped up in front of him. Evidently, Parr had
one MiG pilot's attention because when it tried to
manoeuvre out of his line of fire, it hit the ground and
exploded. The others broke off and headed in the direction
of the Yalu. Despite all of this action in such a short period
of time, Parr's Sabre was never hit, and he was credited
with two MiG-15s destroyed and one damaged (Cover
artwork by Mark Postlethwaite)

CONTENTS

INTRODUCTION

As the Cold War heated up with the communist blockade of Berlin in June 1948, the top priority for the armed forces of the United States was homeland defence. At that time, the first production examples of the F-86A Sabre were just rolling off North American's Inglewood, California, assembly line. The best fighter of its generation, the Sabre was then still eight months away from entering frontline service. And once F-86As began to reach USAF fighter groups, they had one simple mission to perform – to defend North America from attack by Soviet long-range bombers.

As a direct result of this policy, no fighter groups outside of the continental United States had received the superior Sabre by the time North Korean T-34-85 tanks rolled south across the 38th Parallel and headed for Seoul on 25 June 1950. Despite this act of aggression having caught the US military, and its South Korean, allies by surprise, the USAF in particular was confident that it could secure aerial supremacy over the battlefield with its Lockheed F-80 Shooting Stars, which were based in nearby Japan. After all, the North Korean People's Air Force (NKPAF) was equipped exclusively with World War 2-vintage piston-engined aircraft supplied by the Soviet Union.

For the first five months of the war, the F-80s did indeed dominate North Korean skies, prevailing over the handful of NKPAF Yak-9/11s, La-7s and Il-10s that were encountered. However, the first sign that the Lockheed fighter's undisputed dominance was soon to come to an end came during the afternoon of 1 November 1950. Two F-51 Mustang pilots of the 18th Fighter-Bomber Group (FBG) spotted a pair of swept-wing fighters near the Yalu River. One week later, 1Lt Russell J Brown of the F-80C-equipped 16th Fighter Squadron/51st Fighter Wing claimed the world's first jet-versus-jet victory when he downed one of six silver swept-wing MiG-15s that had jumped a flight of F-51Ds.

Despite this first success for the Shooting Star, it quickly became obvious that the MiG-15 was a far superior fighter that boasted a higher speed and greater ceiling than the straight-wing F-80C. Although this engagement proved that the Shooting Star could cope for now, increasing numbers of MiG-15s would soon challenge the air superiority that United Nations' forces had enjoyed since the conflict had commenced. Eager to prevent this from happening, the Far East Air Force (FEAF), which controlled all USAF assets in-theatre, made an urgent request to the Air Force High Command that it immediately be sent F-86 Sabres. Within 72 hours of the first all-jet dogfight having taken place, orders had been cut that would see the USAF's second Sabre fighter group sent to Korea.

Furthermore, Strategic Air Command's best fighter escort wing (equipped with F-84E Thunderjets) would also be committed to combat to help relieve some of the pressure being exerted on the F-80 units that were flying close air support, interdiction and fighter escort missions.

The F-86 unit flagged for deployment to the war zone was the 4th FW, which had been only the second wing to receive Sabres in March 1949. Within hours of being told that it was Korea-bound, the unit had despatched 49 jets to Naval Air Station (NAS) North Island, in San Diego, and 26 aircraft to San Francisco, where the F-86s were quickly loaded onto an aircraft carrier and civilian-owned fast tankers as deck cargo, destined for Japan. By mid-December, aircraft, servicing equipment and personnel were in-theatre, the jets subsequently being flown to Kimpo Air Base, near Seoul.

For the next 31 months, the 4th FW would play a central part in the struggle for aerial supremacy over North Korea. Much of this fighting would take place in the condensed airspace in the northwestern corner of the Korean Peninsula known as 'MiG Alley'. Indeed, USAF statistics published soon after the war had ended stated that 90 per cent of all MiG-15s engaged south of the Yalu River were encountered in 'MiG Alley'.

As the deeds of the Sabre pilots resonated east across the Pacific, the US media began to pick up on the 'jet ace race' that was being fought out over North Korea. The reporting of the Sabre pilots' exploits struck a chord with the general public that had not been seen in America since the days of Gen Claire L Chennault's 'Flying Tigers' in China a decade earlier. Much of the fighting was being done by the 4th FW, and some 23 of the 39 Sabre aces to emerge from the Korean War hailed from the wing. This volume chronicles their story.

THE NEED FOR SPEED

When the 4th FW received its orders to head to Korea on 11 November 1950, the wing found itself having to gather up aircraft, personnel and equipment spread across three different locations. The 4th had been operating jets from three east coast airfields – its headquarters and the 334th FS were based at New Castle County Airport, Delaware, the 335th FS called Andrews AFB, Virginia, home, and the 336th FS was flying out of Dover AFB, also in Delaware. The wing had spread its units between these bases in August 1950.

Manned primarily by combat veterans from World War 2, and boasting an enviable wartime record from its service with the Eighth Air Force in the UK, the 4th FW had already achieved a few 'firsts' with jet fighters. It was the first active jet fighter unit to operate from the east coast, following its switch from F-51Ds to F-80Cs in March 1947, and in May 1949, just two months after receiving its first F-86As, the 4th won first place in the jet class at the USAF Gunnery Meet in Las Vegas. In November 1950, the wing would add to this list by becoming the first unit to deploy for combat with the Sabre.

When the 4th FW received word from USAF Chief of Staff Gen Hoyt S Vandenberg that it was to prepare for immediate movement to the Far East, the wing had less than a week to prepare itself. On 15 November wing personnel and the 334th and 335th FSs flew into NAS North Island in preparation for the fast trip to Japan aboard the aircraft carrier USS *Cape Esperance* (CVE-88). With the vessel's flightdeck full of Sabres, the 336th FS was forced to fly to McClelland AFB, near San Francisco, and have its jets barged to Oakland, where they were loaded aboard four fast tankers as deck cargo. The commercial vessels departed shortly before the

Operated by the Military Sea Transportation Service as a dedicated aircraft transport vessel, the former World War 2 escort carrier USS *Cape Esperance* (CVE-88) carried F-86As for two of the 4th FW's three squadrons from California to Japan in November-December 1950. It took the carrier 13 days to make the voyage across the Pacific from San Diego to Kisarazu (*John Henderson*)

The 4th FW's Sabres are seen sitting on the crowded flightdeck of *Cape Esperance* soon after the vessel's arrival at the Yokosuka navy yard. Note the trio of F6F-5 Hellcats in the left foreground (*North American*)

North American provided expert help in the field with their small army of Technical Representatives, who helped keep the Sabres in the air throughout their tenure in the Korean War. The individual in the black baseball cap is John Henderson, who travelled to the war zone with the 4th FW as part of the team supporting the F-86A. To his left is future 51st FW 'tech rep' James R Moddrell (*John Henderson*)

carrier, and the ships were at sea for approximately 15 days prior to arriving at their final destination of Yokosuka, just south of Tokyo.

John Henderson was North American's senior technical representative sent with the 4th FW to Japan, and he commented on the early technical maladies that beset the wing once it reached the Far East;

'The 4th experienced some serious problems once the Sabres were off-loaded in Japan. The salt spray from the heavy seas that were encountered during the Pacific crossing had caused widespread corrosion between the dissimilar metals of the F-86's airfoils. All aircraft exposed to the elements on the carrier's flightdeck and aboard the tankers had been affected. Fuel contamination from softened fuel quantity transmitter cork floats in the wing cells themselves also caused problems. Treating the corrosion alone delayed the wing by a week in reaching Korea.

'Although the technical problems were soon overcome, the wing was still struggling to find available space for its Sabres at the small bases in South Korea. All usable airfields were already jam packed with fighter-bombers (F-80s and F-51s), and the heavy transport aircraft were beating up the PSP (pierced-steel planking) runways. The only air base in South Korea that could serve the needs of the Sabres was Kimpo. And only 32 jets (of the 75 on strength with the wing), known as Detachment A, could initially be operated from Korea due to the austere facilities on-site. Our primary base of operations would temporarily remain in Japan at Johnson AB.

'The December move from Johnson AB to Kimpo AB was essentially carried out by the 336th FS in the main. This was primarily because the unit's jets had arrived in Japan a few days earlier than *Cape Esperance*, which had been slowed by a drive shaft problem as it crossed the Pacific. This meant that the 336th had already restored a number of its jets to flying status at Johnson AB, and was organising itself for combat, when its two sister squadrons finally arrived. Seven 336th jets were duly flown to Kimpo on 15 December, the lead aircraft being piloted by group CO, and World War 2 ace,

Col John C Meyer. Additional aircraft were flown in following an improvement in the weather until Detachment A finally reached its full strength of 32 Sabres. We now had aircraft and pilots from all three squadrons ready to fly combat missions.

'Due to the cold temperatures we encountered in Korea, the 125 maintenance personnel in Korea experienced great difficulties when it came to servicing and rearming the jets. There was an assortment of systems failures during those early days of combat operations, including drop tank problems, sticking aileron boost control valves, lagging engines in flight, turbine (wheel) blade tip erosion, reduced canopy visibility and an assortment of hydraulic leaks. There were also several cases of frost bitten fingers for the groundcrew working out in the open, and it was so cold that a bucket of water would freeze just eight feet from the tent stove that was going full blast!'

Despite wrestling with extreme weather conditions, and the impact it had on their jets, the personnel of Detachment A remained focused on their primary mission – maintaining air superiority over North Korea, no matter what the cost. The Sabre pilots also flew a handful of fighter-bomber escort and weather reconnaissance missions over northwest Korea. The 4th FW soon got used to this daily combat routine in-theatre from Kimpo, which remained unchanged, bar a short period of basing from Suwon and Taegu ABs during the early months of 1951.

F-86A-5 48-297 of the 334th FS has its engine warmed up on the Kimpo AB flightline on Christmas Day morning after a bitterly cold night out in the open. Note the leftover snow from a previous storm. Amongst the initial batch of Sabres sent to Korea, 48-297 was eventually written off on 11 July 1951 when its pilot failed to recover the jet from a spin during a training flight from Johnson AB (*John Henderson*)

Weather conditions were always a problem at the forward operating bases such as Taegu and Suwon. The PSP runways and taxiways at both sites was soon left in poor condition due to the dozens of heavy transport aircraft that shuttled through the airfields on a daily basis. These 4th FW pilots are trying to make it out to the flightline in early 1951 during a late winter thaw (*Jack Wingo*)

INTO COMBAT

Records state that the 4th FW's initial temporary duty to the Far East saw a total of 131 officers and 413 enlisted men make the move. These figures included pilots and support personnel. The responsibility placed on them was considerable, for they were about to enter an uncertain arena in which the enemy's capabilities were relatively unknown. Indeed, as they settled into their

temporary bases in Japan, the question on every pilot's mind was just how tough would the new MiG-15 be, and what were its characteristics, especially its strengths and weaknesses?

Intelligence sources were of little help. All they had to go on were camera-gun pictures and sketchy descriptions provided by F-51 and F-80 pilots who had usually viewed the aircraft from afar. One thing was known for certain though. The MiG-15 could climb faster than anything seen before – an ominous portent of its capabilities, especially when flown by an experienced pilot. And another thing – the MiGs would be flying just a short distance from their Manchurian bases, leaving them with plenty of fuel for a fight. The F-86s, on the other hand, would have travelled about 200 miles by the time they arrived over 'MiG Alley'. They would be low on fuel, for even when fitted with two 120-gallon external drop tanks, the Sabre's combat radius was only about 500 miles.

On 15 December 4th FW CO Col John C Meyer led a detachment of F-86As from Johnson to Kimpo. Wing records state that at 1550 hrs that same day, seven Sabres flown by pilots of Detachment A left Kimpo for the North Korea-Manchuria border. Although this flight was performed primarily for orientation and familiarisation purposes, it represented the Sabre's first venture over enemy-held territory. The mission passed without event, as no MiGs were sighted, and another patrol scheduled for the following day was cancelled due to bad weather. The first clash was postponed, but not for long.

On 17 December 336th FS CO Lt Col Bruce N Hinton led a flight of F-86s on a combat air patrol along the Yalu River. It did not take long for them to arouse the enemy's attention, and the flight's No 2 man warned of four bogies flying in a southeasterly direction toward the Sabres. The No 3 pilot called that

The air bases in Japan were in far better condition than those in South Korea, as this photograph of the 334th FS's F-86A-5 49-1193 at Johnson AB in early 1951 proves. This airfield was used as a major staging area for the 4th FW prior to its units heading to Korea for combat (John Henderson)

A high-scoring Mustang ace with the 352nd FG in World War 2, Col John C Meyer, seen here on the left, went to Korea with the 4th FW as its group commander. This photograph was taken at Suwon AB in March 1951, Meyer discussing tactics with some of his pilots prior to flying yet another mission. He claimed two MiG-15 kills (Al Beaty)

they were swept-wing jets. Hinton subsequently described that historic first encounter;

'The No 2 pilot in our flight observed four bogies coming from Sinuiju, and our No 3 confirmed the sighting as swept-wing types. They were at approximately 18,000 ft and we were up at 25,000 ft. We proceeded to turn into the enemy aircraft, diving all the way. The MiGs were in battle formation, and they immediately went into a climbing right trail. We continued our turn, and we began to out turn them while pulling about five Gs. At that time the enemy formation seemed to lose integrity as they observed us coming in, and they levelled out on a heading parallel with the Yalu River.

'I picked out their lead element to attack, and when I was at a distance of about 4000 ft their external tanks came off. Checking my airspeed, I moved into the "six o'clock" position of the MiG element. At that time, I noticed that we were redlined at 0.95 Mach. My Mach meter was quite a way past the red line, and it was the fastest I had ever flown an F-86.

'Our Nos 3 and 4 broke off and began pursuing the other MiG element. I picked the closest one, which was their No 2, and put my pipper squarely on where its main fuel tank should have been and continued to close. My radio transmitter had gone out, but I could hear the other pilots in my flight talking on the radio, and as I got to within firing range I stopped hearing any transmissions. When I had closed to within 1500 ft of the MiG I opened fire with a short burst. I noted numerous strikes with my API (armour-piercing incendiary) rounds. They found their mark, and I spotted fluid/smoke leaking from several holes in the MiG's wing – this was either fuel leaking from internal tanks or smoke from my burning API rounds.

'It was at this point that I realised I did not have my wingman with me, and had probably lost him when we made the break, as no one was able to hear my radio transmission.

'All of a sudden, the pilot of my MiG popped his speed brakes and then retracted them immediately, which increased my rate of closure, so I put my pipper on his tailpipe to get at his engine. My reasoning was that the cold air and non-volatile jet fuel might inhibit burning or explosion of his fuel tanks. Before I could squeeze off another burst, my Sabre began violently twisting and bouncing in the MiG's jet wash, so I slid off to the inside slightly, clearing the turbulence. At this point, my range

336th FS pilots 'chew the fat' whilst enjoying a cigarette break at Suwon AB in the early spring of 1951. They will soon head to their jets and take-off on a combat air patrol over 'MiG Alley'. On the far left is squadron commander Lt Col Bruce Hinton, who claimed the 4th FW's first MiG-15 kill on 15 December 1950 (*John Henderson*)

This was one of the early scoreboards kept by the 335th FS at Suwon. The red stars are confirmed kills, whilst the others are damaged or probable victories. James Jabara, who was the 4th's first Sabre ace, has his name on this list, despite the fact that he was actually assigned to the 334th FS. This is explained by the fact that the 335th FS was the parent unit at Suwon in the spring of 1951, and pilots from the 334th and 336th FSs would rotate through the base from Johnson AB (*Richard Merian*)

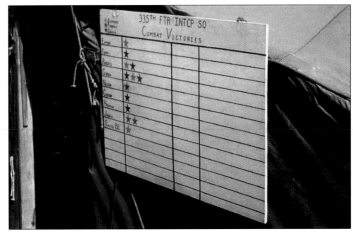

This planform photograph of Lt Col Hinton's F-86A-5 49-1180 *Squanee* was taken by an RB-45 Tornado reconnaissance jet whilst flying on a mission over North Korea in early 1951. Hinton was leading a flight of four escorting Sabres at the time. The distinctive black and white stripes were applied to all F-86s in-theatre in 1950-51, making the jet easy to spot from great distances (*Edward Kendrex*)

The MiG-15 was equipped with 23 mm and 37 mm cannon, whose slow rate of fire usually meant that an alert F-86 pilot could evade most rounds. However, if the Sabre was hit by a 37 mm shell in particular, it usually meant heavy damage or loss of the aircraft altogether. This 334th FS F-86A took a large-calibre cannon round in the flaps, but still made it back to base (*Phil Anderson*)

was only about 800 ft, and I gave him a long burst. Pieces flew off and his tailpipe was filled with smoke. A second later, a long plume of flame lengthened out of the opening. His airspeed dropped and I put out my speed brakes and throttled back to idle, but I was still gaining on him. We hung there in the sky, turning left, with my F-86 tight against his underside in a show formation, separated by just five feet.

'Moving back into a firing position once again, I shot off another long burst that resulted in more flames exiting the tailpipe. These enveloped the entire MiG, which suddenly did a reverse turn and flipped onto its back, before slowing down and rapidly losing altitude in a steep dive. The smoke trail went straight toward the ground approximately ten miles southeast of the Yalu, below 10,000 ft. No explosion was seen.'

All told, Hinton had fired 1500 rounds to bag his MiG, and he celebrated his success with a victory roll at 500 knots over Kimpo upon his return to base.

While he was scoring the F-86's first confirmed kill, two other 336th FS Sabre pilots had engaged the second element of MiGs that had initially been spotted. They zeroed in on the No 4 jet, and pushing their airspeed to 0.98 Mach, were slowly gaining on the communist fighter. The MiG pilot then made a left turn and headed straight down toward the Yalu, accelerating rapidly. The Sabre pilots were forced to quickly take a fleeting shot at the fighter from long distance, and one of them reported seeing an aircraft pouring smoke and fire, heading straight for the ground – Hinton's MiG.

The first major confrontation had ended in favour of the F-86, but the battle between the two jets was just beginning. The 4th FIW's pilots now knew something else about their opponent – when the MiG dropped its nose and accelerated, it was extremely fast. Indeed, in this first engagement two machines had used their speed to escape unscathed.

Five days later, on the morning of 22 December, the stage was set for a much larger duel. Two F-86 flights were cruising at 35,000 ft when they encountered several MiGs, and the ensuing dogfight was brief, but intense. It would also be the first time that the Americans experienced the effect of the opposition's heavy calibre guns. Capt Bach was caught from behind as he broke hard right, 37 mm rounds hitting his wing root and causing his F-86A (49-1176) to begin a series of violent snap-rolls. Bach punched out and became a prisoner of war (PoW). This was the conflict's first Sabre combat loss.

But Bach's capture was soon avenged that afternoon in what would prove to be one of the F-86's most successful fights, considering the odds. Only eight jets participated in this combat air patrol, but once the dust had settled their pilots had scored six confirmed MiG kills.

The flight leaders on this occasion were two of the most experienced pilots in the business – Col John C Meyer and Lt Col Glenn T Eagleston, both of whom were high-scor-

ing Mustang aces from World War 2. At the climax of the battle there were elements of MiG-15s scattered from 32,000 ft down to tree-top level. As fuel was running low, some of the F-86s started working their way back to the south. One element spotted two MiGs at 9000 ft and could not pass up the opportunity this offered. Within a minute both enemy jets had been shot down. The victorious Sabres were led by Eagleston, with Lt John Odiorne as his wingman. Meyer had one of the more spectacular kills that afternoon when, flying at 20,000 ft, he got in a high-deflection burst at a fast-moving MiG. His rounds impacted all over the aircraft, causing it to disintegrate.

Several facts emerged from the subsequent debriefing. First, the importance of the two-ship element, even in fast-moving high-mach fights, was clear. It also seemed that most MiG pilots tried to set up their firing positions from the rear, but in each case the Sabre wingmen were able to keep their 'shooters' informed, enabling the F-86s to emerge

Capt James Roberts, 1Lt Ward Hitt, Lt Col John Meyer and 1Lt Arthur O'Connor relive their one-sided clash with MiG-15s on 22 December 1950. Roberts, Meyer and O'Connor all claimed kills (*Ward Hitt*)

Yet another World War 2 ace to enjoy early success with the 4th FW in Korea in 1950-51 was Lt Col Glenn Eagleston, who flew this F-86A-5 (49-1281) at various times during his combat tour. He claimed two MiG-15 kills, one probable and seven damaged, with one of the latter coming in this very jet on 6 April 1951. 49-1281 was lost in combat with MiG-15s on 25 June 1951 (*Australian War Memorial*)

without loss. Kills were credited to Meyer, Eagleston and Cdr Paul Pugh (a US Navy exchange pilot), all from 4th FW HQ, Capt James Roberts (335th) and Lts Arthur O'Connor (336th) and Odiorne (334th).

On the final day of December, the 4th sent 33 Sabres to patrol the Yalu around the town of Sinuiju. These aircraft were split into two different flights which were staggered in timing so that as the first ran low on fuel the second would come on station. Although the weather was perfect, the MiG-15s stayed on the ground. This trend continued into 1951.

This photograph, taken in the late spring of 1951, shows the dispersal area at Suwon AB enjoying a dry spell after a harsh wet winter. The 4th FW's Sabres were still rotating between Japan and South Korea at this time. However, in the early summer the wing moved in its entirety to Suwon AB, and then on to Kimpo AB several weeks later (*James Dennison*)

Group records state that in the final two weeks of December 1950, 234 sorties had been logged, and MiGs had been engaged 76 times. The results were eight officially credited kills and two probables for the loss of one F-86.

Detachment A's existence at Kimpo (and also Suwon) ended on the afternoon of 2 January 1951 when the Chinese advance threatened UN bases in the northern sectors of South Korea. All tactical aircraft units, and personnel, were evacuated to the Japanese bases at Itazuke and Johnson, the 4th going to the latter site. Enemy forces were very close to over-running Kimpo when the last USAF units pulled out.

After initially returning to Johnson AB, the 4th FW was finally able to make tentative steps back into Korea in early 1951 when the Chinese advance had been halted. The wing started by launching missions from Taegu AB, which was some distance south of Kimpo. Operations were severely hampered by a general lack of external fuel tanks and the greater flying distance to and from 'MiG Alley', and the two combined to make it almost impossible for the wing to conduct productive air patrols over northwestern Korea.

With full scale Combat Air Patrols having to be temporarily abandoned, the 4th's senior officers began to look around for other ways to keep the wing in the fight until a more suitable airfield could be secured. One role that was briefly adopted was the air-to-ground mission. The reasoning behind this was that the Sabre was much faster than the F-84, which in turn meant that it could get to and from its target quicker than any other fighter-bomber then in-theatre. It also gave pilots more combat time, which they were lacking due to the lull in 'MiG Alley' missions. While the wing did not fly these fighter-bomber sorties for long, it planted the seed for future close air support missions by F-86Fs that would exceed all expectations during the final six months of the Korean War.

On 17 January 1951, combat operations with the Sabre returned to Korea when the 335th FS sent a handful of its jets to Taegu AB. Records show that between 17 and 31 January, the number of aircraft available for operations by the squadron varied from four to eight. Pilots were rotated frequently so that as many as possible could gain valuable combat experience. From Taegu, the unit flew several types of mission – armed reconnaissance, close support under 'Mosquito' control (forward air controllers in AT-6 Texans) and combat air patrols. The 4th FW's official history states that some missions were flown with a full 0.50-cal load only, or with full ammunition, two 5-inch High-Velocity Aerial Rockets under the wings and maximum fuel, which included the external tanks.

One of the 335th FS pilots rotated through Taegu in January was 2Lt Alonzo 'Lon' J Walter. A young and relatively inexperienced F-86 pilots with less than 100 hours total flying time in the Sabre when he accompanied the 4th FW to Korea in late 1950, he had not been sent to Kimpo with Detachment A. Eager to see combat, Walter was one of the new pilots that were fortunate enough to fly these fighter-bomber missions;

'The pilots that had flown from Kimpo in December were the most experienced in the 4th FG, and were perhaps the most combat experienced jet pilots in the world at that point in time. For new pilots like me, we were left at Johnson AB and told to work on building up our hours in the Sabre. Unfortunately, there were no facilities in Japan to conduct live air-to-air or air-to-ground gunnery, so when a small detachment from the 4th went to Taegu, all of us youngsters were desperate for a piece of the action, whether we were deemed to have adequate experience or not!'

'I was very lucky to be one of the pilots that went with the detachment. We shared quarters with some of the F-80 pilots from the 49th FBG. It was bitterly cold, and the pot-bellied stove worked overtime to keep our huts livable. My first ever combat mission was led by veteran Capt Martin Johansen. The rest of us were all second lieutenants with about the same amount of F-86 time, and none of us had ever fired the jet's guns or shot a rocket.

'Capt Johansen briefed us on all the mission details – I was to fly in the No 4 position. Our aircraft were armed with 1200 rounds of .50-cal API, just in case we encountered enemy tanks, and two 5-inch HVARs, plus the usual 120-gallon external tanks.

'After take-off from Taegu, we were to proceed over to the Suwon area and contact a forward air controller (FAC). Climbing up to an altitude of 20,000 ft, the flight only took a few minutes, during which time we got our first good look at the snowy, mountainous Korean terrain.

'We were told by the airborne controller that there was a large concentration of Chinese troops in foxholes on a hillside overlooking our former base at Suwon. The FAC fired a white phosphorous smoke rocket which marked the target. He then cleared us to direct our guns and ordnance into the vicinity of his smoke. On our first passes we would

His jet almost ready for its next duel with communist MiGs over the Yalu, a 335th FS crew chief polishes the windscreen of F-86A 48-261 at Kimpo AB in the early summer of 1951. This early-build Sabre survived its tour of duty in Korea and was eventually sent home to serve with the 3595th Training Wing at Nellis AFB (*Phil Anderson*)

use our 0.50-cal guns, and when we ran low on ammunition we would fire our rockets. We fell into trail formation and set up a gunnery pattern very much like a small rectangular traffic pattern.

'For the life of me, I could not see any foxholes and no sign of life anywhere. I watched Capt Johansen roll in and fire on the hillside, followed by the other two pilots in my flight. I reasoned that as I dived towards the target, I'd probably be able to make out what it was that I was shooting at, but this did not happen!'

The four Sabre pilots made three gunnery passes at the area designated by the FAC. When they had finished, flight lead told them to set up for the first rocket pass. Moments after the No 3 had fired his projectiles, the FAC called out 'Look at that!' Enemy troops were leaving their foxholes and running up the side of the hill. 2Lt Walter was still having trouble seeing any movement from the target area, but he went ahead and fired. As he pulled up, his wingman stated that his rockets had hit right in the centre of the fleeing troops. The FAC, call-sign 'Mosquito Poison', congratulated the pilots on the accuracy of their shooting as the four jets headed back to Taegu.

In looking back on that mission, 2Lt Walter recalled;

'As I was shooting ordnance for the first time, I had no concept of judging range. I simply bored right in until I thought I was at about the right distance and opened fire. Looking back after many years of experience, I now know that I must have been well out of range on each pass. The other young pilots in the flight most likely did the same, but it's hard to miss a hill!

'We must have done something right, however, as the Chinese troops poured out of their foxholes and ran up the hill. My guess is that it was the first time that they had

4th FW Sabres share ramp space at Johnson AB with an F-80C from the 41st FS/35th FG in early 1951. This group was also based at Johnson at the time (Robert Botts)

World War 2 ace Col Walker 'Bud' Mahurin joined the 4th FW as group CO in March 1952, having previously claimed 3.5 MiG-15 victories with the 51st FW. One of the best Sabre pilots to see combat in Korea, Mahurin was a strong advocate of the F-86 as a fighter-bomber. He eventually fell victim to communist AAA whilst conducting a low-level attack on North Korean targets on 13 May 1952 and spent the rest of the war as a PoW in Manchuria (USAF)

One of the 4th FW's most photographed Sabres, this F-86E was assigned to the 336th FS and flown by World War 2 ace Col Walker 'Bud' Mahurin whilst both Deputy CO and CO of the 4th FG. Mahurin was shot down by AAA whilst at the controls of F-86E-10 51-2789 on 13 May 1952, and he spent the rest of the war as a PoW. 51-2747 survived the war, however, and was subsequently posted to the 35th FG (*William Thomas*)

seen an F-86 – the only other jets they were familiar with were F-80s and F-84s. We were carrying external tanks, and they might have mistaken them for napalm. Figuring that we were saving these fearful weapons until last, they made a run for it. During our debriefing, one of our intelligence guys came in and said the FAC had reported over 200 enemy troops killed in our attack.'

Only a few more of these air-to-ground missions were flown from Taegu prior to the Sabres returning to Johnson AB on 31 January. The Korean base was exclusively equipped with PSP, which quickly proved to be less than ideal for F-86 operations, especially in the poor winter weather. The 4th's brief flirtation with air-to-ground missions was not deemed an outstanding success, but at least it had proven that the Sabre was a capable fighter-bomber.

More than 12 months would pass before the wing would fly close air support and interdiction missions once again. In May 1952, group CO, and World War 2 ace, Col Walker 'Bud' Mahurin set put to prove just how capable a fighter-bomber the Sabre was. Several missions were flown with good success, the jets typically carrying two 500- or 1000-lb bombs.

On 13 May, Mahurin (who had already claimed 3.5 MiG-15 kills during his time in Korea) led aloft a formation of four F-86Es loaded with two 1000-lb general purpose bombs apiece. Unable to carry external fuel tanks because of this maximum effort load, they struck targets in North Korea that were within their limited range. Col Mahurin's jet was hit by accurate ground fire during one of his attacking runs and he was forced to eject. He spent the rest of the war as a PoW.

By this point in time it was evident that the F-86 would be an excellent fighter-bomber, and in July 1952 the USAF gave North American the green light to begin modifying new F-models as they were coming off the line so that they could perform this mission. By the end of 1952, the 8th (F-80s) and 18th FBWs (F-51s) were slated to begin conversion onto

17

MEETING THE MiG CHALLENGE

By early 1951, RF-80 tactical reconnaissance missions along the Yalu were revealing an almost daily increase in the number of MiGs parked on the Manchurian air bases of Antung and Mukden, yet these jets were not coming south of the river in greater numbers. UN Intelligence theorised that the units operating the aircraft were just biding their time for an all-out assault, or that these bases were key training grounds for MiG operations. Either way, the jets posed a potential problem for the FEAF, and the 4th FW in particular.

At this stage of the war, the number of Sabres in-theatre was just keeping pace with the attrition rate. This meant that if a large force of MiGs attacked UN fighter-bombers, the F-86s providing top cover would be hard-pressed to handle the threat. On 6 March, the 334th FS began staging patrols out of Suwon for the first time since it had been forced to evacuate South Korea on 2 January. Although the base had just a single concrete runway surrounded by a quagmire of mud, by the end of March the entire squadron was flying routine maximum-strength patrols, but encountering no increased enemy fighter activity.

Despite the Sabres' presence, dealing with the B-29s and fighter-bombers was still regarded by the MiG units as their top priority because of the damage being inflicted on high-value assets in North Korea. As a result, the bombers found themselves becoming more vulnerable to concentrated MiG attacks during January and February 1951, and daylight missions were soon considered too dangerous for unescorted piston-engined medium and heavy bombers such as the B-26 and B-29.

The 4th FW was immediately given the job of escorting the vulnerable 'heavies', and it soon became embroiled in some of its most complex and vicious fights with the MiGs. Usually, Sabre top cover was coordinated not only with the bomber stream, but also with the slower fighter-

Three flights of F-86As taxi out onto the runway at Taegu in the spring of 1951. Such a sight indicated that the 4th FW was mounting a squadron-strength patrol over the Yalu River. Maintenance personnel were hard-pressed at this time to get so many F-86s serviceable on a daily basis due to a chronic shortage of spare parts in the Far East (*Robert Andrews*)

bombers that were attacking targets close by. With the F-86 screen having to provide protection for both strikes simultaneously, these combat air patrols proved difficult to plan, with the fighters' timing on station being of critical importance. Often, the Sabres arrived slightly early or late, and sometimes the B-29s were not on time. But they could always rely on the MiGs being airborne, ready to oppose the bombers.

A typical mission flown during this period took place on 12 April, when a bomber formation from Okinawa was assigned to attack major targets in the Sinuiju area, including a critical railway bridge. Thirty-nine B-29s were escorted by F-84s at and below their altitude, with F-86s high above in the top cover position. As the bombers began their run on the bridge, all hell broke loose when at least 70 MiG-15s swarmed in from the north. The Sabre pilots had their hands full due to the sheer size of the communist formations participating in the attacks, for the enemy had never been encountered in such numbers before. It proved to be a costly learning experience for the MiG pilots, however, as they lost ten of their number within minutes.

Once the MiGs penetrated the F-86 cover, they literally ran into a 'wall of lead' thrown up by the B-29 gunners. This was probably the first time that these pilots had attacked a big bomber formation, and they paid the price, for six of the confirmed MiG kills fell to the B-29s' 0.50-cal turrets. Another four jets were gunned down by 4th FW Sabres drawn from both the 334th and 336th FSs, MiGs falling to Meyer, Hinton, Capt Howard Lane and future first Sabre ace Capt James Jabara. In this engagement, Jabara scored his third kill, and he was now just a month away from the coveted fifth.

TACTICS

As Sabre pilots began to learn more and more about the capabilities of their foes in their MiG-15, the tactics that were devised by the experienced heads leading the three fighter squadrons in-theatre were passed on to the next generation of pilots arriving at Suwon from advanced jet training schools in the USA. The integrity of the four-ship flight and the two-ship element were of utmost importance. The value put on each pilot's safety, and their aircraft, could never bet set too high, and these rules were meant to be 'force multipliers' that increased the chances of survival. This in turn meant that pilots could return to the fight again and again.

There was one cardinal rule that the 4th FW 'bent' only a few times. This pertained to when visual contact was made with the MiGs and external tanks were jettisoned. If by some chance one or both of the tanks failed to release from and F-86, that aircraft would immediately return to base with his wingman. A hung tank would greatly diminish the speed and manoeuvrability of the F-86, so this rule was seldom questioned – even if it meant cutting a flight of four in half.

The most famous 'exception' to this rule occurred on 20 May 1951, when Capt James Jabara set out on patrol with four kills under his belt. That day, an unusually large fight was brewing over 'MiG Alley'. Patrols were scattered when friendly radar picked up 50 MiG-15s crossing the river, and a call went out for all 36 Sabres in the area to converge on the enemy from all directions. The fight was on.

Capt James Jabara is carried from his F-86 by fellow Sabre pilots upon his return to Suwon following his 'ace-making' sortie during the late afternoon of 20 May 1951 (*USAF*)

With his feet now back on terra firma, Jabara accepts the congratulations of other Sabre pilots in front of 335th FS F-86A-5 49-1210. Note the USAF photographer hastily changing a roll of film in his camera in the foreground! Everyone wanted to shake hands and take a photograph of America's first jet ace on this truly historical occasion (*Leo Fournier*)

Jabara attempted to drop his external tanks when the sighting was called, but one hung up, putting him at a distinct disadvantage. Rather than obey the unwritten rule and leave the area with his wingman, he chose to attack. When the brief fight ended, three MiG-15s had been destroyed, with Jabara claiming two of them for his fifth and sixth kills. He had just become the first American jet ace.

Although there were probably several incidents where pilots continued to fight on with a hung tank, they were few and far between. 335th FS pilot 1Lt David P Proctor recalled a mission that he was on that saw a similar situation arise;

'We had been patrolling deep in MiG territory without seeing much action. Just as we turned back to the south, we spotted a flight of enemy jets just north of Pyongyang. I gave the word to jettison tanks, but my wingman couldn't get both of his off. We were in a position where we had to take the MiGs on, so I gave him permission to continue with the bounce. The reasoning behind this was I knew that he could not keep up with me, so at least I could protect him while he was the shooter. Our biggest problem was a second flight of MiGs that we had not seen behind some clouds. They appeared just as a jet in the original flight began to smoke heavily and shed some pieces from its fuselage.

'Breaking hard into the second flight as my wingman rejoined me, I immediately attacked the enemy flight leader. We exchanged a head-on firing pass and wound up in a steep climbing scissors. The much lighter MiG eventually spun me out, but, fortunately, he did not press home his advantage.

'We recovered back at Kimpo AB to discover that my wingman had been hit in the vertical stabiliser from approximately 30 degrees off the head-on. There was some consternation at HQ level, since Fifth Air Force policy prohibited engagements with a hung tank unless attacked. I think the only thing that saved me from harsh discipline was the two kills that Jim Jabara had made several weeks earlier in a jet with a hung tank.'

THE ENEMY

The fact that the Soviet and Warsaw Pact air regiments that saw action in MiG-15s in Korea gained their combat experience the hard way is well known. The communists would often pull entire units out of combat and replace them with new ones that had little or no experience in fighting F-86s.

In an effort to improve the standard of local North Korean and Chinese pilots, the Russians set up a major training centre spread across several air bases north of the Yalu River, and within easy flying distance of northwestern North Korea ('MiG Alley'). The heart of this operation was at Antung AB.

Students under instruction were able to utilise the excellent high

altitude performance of the MiG-15 by cruising above F-86 formations, safe in the knowledge that the Sabre's service ceiling was barely 45,000 ft. Staying at 50,000 ft+, the new MiG pilots could observe the tactics used by both sides in fights that were initiated by the more experienced communist aviators (nicknamed 'Honchos' by the Americans) far below them.

It is believed that the Russians began establishing a first-class training facility at Antung in the early autumn of 1950, just as North Korean fortunes in the conflict began to deteriorate. From what seemed like a great victory for the communist forces in August, the Inchon landings by the US Marine Corps on 15 September quickly put the entire Korean peninsula within the grasp of the democratic south.

The MiG build up north of the Yalu River evidently started to gain momentum at this time, the communists perhaps planning to turn South Korea into one huge fighter base that could have posed a grave threat to Japan should they have succeeded in capturing the entire country. This never happened, of course, but the expansion of the air bases within the Antung Complex was both real and ongoing for the duration of the Korean War. Countering this threat placed a heavy load of responsibility on the 4th FW, and it carried the burden alone for almost a year.

334th FS pilot 1Lt Ray Nyls remembers discussing the communists' training cycle with his squadronmates;

'It seemed to us that the MiG pilots were undergoing some sort of combat readiness school up around Antung. Their aggressive stance would run in cycles of about six weeks. At first they seemed timid and would sit up at high altitude in the sun and study our formations, but they never attacked us. Then they would become bolder, and an occasional flight would drop down for a quick firing pass at us and then accelerate right back up out of our reach. At the end of their training cycle, they would come in on us and really mix it up. A few days later, the cycle would start all over again. When they did choose to go head-to-head with us once their training cycle had finished, we soon found that their piloting skills were still well below ours, however.

'I recall one mission during a period when they were only coming at us one flight (four aircraft) at a time. An F-86 from my flight came

Two 4th FW Sabres close in on a fleeing MiG-15 as its pilot desperately attempts to make it back to the safety of the northern banks of the Yalu River. Later stills from this reel of gun camera footage showed that the communist pilot failed in his bid to escape (*Bill Graski*)

This particular F-86A was flown in combat by the 336th FS for two years between 1950 and 1952. Having survived this lengthy combat tour, it was shipped back to the USA and issued to the 3595th Training Wing at Nellis AFB in August 1953 (*Jack Wingo*)

in behind an element of two MiGs and shot down the leader. Seconds later, the No 2 pilot punched out without a shot being fired at him. He made no effort to evade. It was the first time we had witnessed anything like that, and it made us wonder what was going through the wingman's mind just prior to ejecting.

'Years later, I had an opportunity to talk with a MiG pilot that had flown against us, and he confirmed a fact that we all suspected – the Soviet fighter had a very nasty stall characteristic when it was pulled too tightly into a high-speed turn. The pilot would experience stick reversal because the jet did not have hydraulic controls, causing it to do a sharp turn that would "Class-26" (write off) the aircraft from excessive strain. We noticed this manoeuvre, and wondered how in the heck they could keep doing that and get away from us. We had the same problem with the older F-86A models, even though they were fitted with hydraulic controls. The latter at least meant that we could usually control stick reversal by applying forward pressure to the controls.'

During the first five months of 1951, the MiG activity and level of pilot experience was fairly predictable. The biggest problem for the 4th was trying to establish a quality airfield in South Korea that could house the entire wing. Once UN ground forces stopped the big Chinese offensive and pushed communist forces back to the 38th Parallel, the facilities at Kimpo AB began to take shape once again.

There were no kills registered in January and February 1951 and only one in March. In April the communist jets became more aggressive, and there were numerous dogfights that included as many as 50+ MiGs at a time. There is no logical explanation for this lull after the wild December 1950 period, except perhaps that the pilots who had engaged the Sabres at this time had been advanced students that still lacked certain skills. And the early losses suffered by the MiG units in combat had meant that the experienced instructors in Manchuria were left scrambling to fill the gaps with new pilots.

Records kept by North American's Technical Representatives serving with the 4th FW during the late spring of 1951 indicate the strain put on all of the maintenance people to keep as many Sabres as possible in the air against ever larger formations of MiGs that were now being encountered over northwest Korea. At this time, there were still a lack of adequate airfields in-theatre to house all of the wing's Sabres, which meant that the 4th was having to operate two squadrons at forward bases and one in reserve back at Johnson AB.

Frequently, a patrol of just 12 to 16 Sabres would be confronted by up to 60 MiGs. And despite their best efforts, the maintenance crews were hampered in their attempts to get more jets aloft because of an ongoing shortage of spare parts which often saw the F-86's in-service rate drop to about 35 per cent on some days. This improved somewhat when more F-86As arrived in Japan in mid 1951, followed by the first E-model jets in early October. A flood of spare parts for the older A-models at around this time finally resulted in dramatically increased service rates, and the number of MiGs being shot down rose accordingly.

The maximum effort being put in by the 4th FW in the spring of 1951 is reflected in the statistics contained within a report published by the FEAF for combat in Korea in the month of May. The wing was charged

A handful of F-86s fell victim to nocturnal attacks performed by NKPAF Po-2 biplanes from June 1951 until war's end. F-86A-5 49-1327 was the first Sabre to be lost to a 'Bed-Check Charlie' attack, the fighter being hit by one of two 25-lb fragmentation bombs dropped on the 335th FS's dispersal area at Suwon at 0130 hrs on 17 June 1951. A further eight Sabres were damaged in the low altitude raid (*Irv Clark*)

Maj Richard D Creighton was the first of three pilots to achieve ace status whilst serving with the 336th FS – the lowest-scoring unit in the 4th FW. Creighton was the fourth Sabre ace of the war, claiming his fifth kill on 27 November 1951 (*USAF*)

with protecting vulnerable fighter-bombers that were flying round the clock in an effort to disrupt a build up of troops and supplies by the Chinese, who were planning a major late spring offensive. The latter was aimed at breaching UN lines which had finally stabilised around the 38th Parallel – where the border between North and South Korea had been pre-war.

During May the 4th flew 3331 sorties totalling an incredible 5314 combat hours over North Korea. This averaged out to 1.5 hours in the air for each Sabre on every sortie. The 335th FS also posted a personal best when its maintenance personnel managed to have all of the squadron's F-86s serviceable for 15 days in a row. The other two squadrons also had strings of five days at a time with 100 per cent serviceability.

Yet despite literally flying the wings off their Sabres, the 4th only posted five kills for the month, compared with 15 in April. Perhaps the constant show of force of F-86s over 'MiG Alley' had kept enemy fighters north of the Yalu River?

All of this changed on the morning of 17 June, when Sabre pilots met a formation of approximately 15 MiG-15s that were flown aggressively, and whose pilots appeared to be well versed in the use of swept-wing fighter tactics. Up until this date, the 4th had occasionally encountered 'honcho' pilots in ones and twos, and such dogfights were long remembered. 'Honchos' usually flew as singletons or in two-ship formations, remaining some distance away from their student charges. Such engagements were the first indication that the number of combat-savvy communist pilots in-theatre was on the rise, and that future MiG hunting might prove to be more difficult.

The fight on the 17th netted one kill for 4th HQ pilot Capt Samuel Pesacreta, with a further six MiGs being listed as damaged. All the F-86s involved returned to Suwon unscathed.

The poor showing for the MiG pilots during this clash did not hamper their will to fight again, for 24 hours later 40+ jets showed up over the Yalu for a duel with 32 F-86s. A fierce dogfight erupted, and for several minutes the sky was filled with silver jets. The communist pilots did not back off, leaving the Sabre pilots with their hands full. When they finally disengaged, five MiG-15s had been shot down for the loss of 334th FS F-86A 49-1307. This aircraft was officially listed as the second Sabre to be downed by a MiG-15 in Korea. Two of the MiG victories were claimed by future aces Maj Richard Creighton and 1Lt Ralph Gibson.

On 19 June the Sabres and MiG-15s went head-to-head once again, with four communist jets being claimed as damaged for the loss of a 336th FS F-86A (49-1298). As with the Sabre lost the previous day, the pilot was not recovered. Although the MiG pilots had failed in their efforts to seize aerial supremacy over the Yalu River from the 4th FW, they had shown a

While a surface attack by MiG-15s was unlikely, the threat of night nuisance raids by anachronistic Po-2s was very real. Things got so bad during the summer of 1951 that the 4th FW requisitioned camouflage netting in order to hide its 650 mph Sabres from Polikarpov biplanes that could barely manage 90 mph with a favourable tail wind! This photograph was taken at Suwon AB in July 1951 (*John Henderson*)

heightened level of combat proficiency, and confidence, that they had failed to display in the past.

There was much discussion within the FEAF at the time as to why the MiG-15 units had acted so aggressively during the second half of June 1951. Senior officers eventually decided that it was probably because the communists were hoping to achieve a modicum of control in the skies over northern Korea so as to allow their vulnerable piston-engined Il-10 ground attack aircraft to be introduced into the action.

Indeed, on the morning of 20 June, the NKPAF sent in several formations of Ilyushins in support of ground forces that were attempting to defeat South Korean troops that were holding the strategically important island of Sinmi-do, 75 miles southeast of Sinuiju. Due to bad luck and bad timing, the effort met with disaster, for en route to their target, the Il-10s flew within sight of a large formation of F-51D Mustangs from the 18th FBG that were attacking nearby ground targets. The intruders were immediately intercepted and two Il-10s shot down, with several others escaping with serious battle damage. For some reason this formation was escorted by piston-engined Yak-9s rather than MiG-15s, and the Yakovlev fighters posed little threat to the veteran Mustang pilots.

WINGMEN

The policies put in place by the wing CO and his squadron commanders in the 4th FW put a premium on experience, which meant that unless a pilot had a certain number of missions (50+) under his belt, he would have to fly in the No 2 or No 4 slots as wingmen to the element or formation leaders. The strict enforcement of such rules resulted in many younger pilots within the wing completing their combat tours without getting the chance to 'mix it up' with the MiGs – engaging enemy fighters was left to the element/formation leaders.

With the exploits of the Sabre aces gaining all the media coverage, the high-scoring pilots' most valuable asset – their wingmen – were often ignored by the press. In a flight of four aircraft, they would be the two pilots with the least combat experience, yet their responsibility was considerable. They had to protect their leaders at any cost. One such wingman was 2Lt Robert W Smith, who did time in F-86As back in the USA before his combat tour. He had the privilege of flying wing for Capt Ralph 'Hoot' Gibson when he got his fifth kill, on 9 September 1951, to become the war's third jet ace. At the time, Smith was still assigned to the 336th FS, but he was flying in a 335th gaggle at the time;

'I remember watching "Hoot" down that MiG-15, and I was probably mesmerised by the sight. His rounds were hitting the MiG, and they made sparkles like some sort of a pinball machine. I thought I was doing a good job keeping his "six o'clock" clear when suddenly I saw telltale balls of fire from a MiG's 37 mm cannon passing over my wing. There were four enemy fighters right behind me!

'I immediately called out for "Hoot" to break, but he was too engrossed to be interrupted. His only reply was "Can you handle it?" I told him I was going to break off, and immediately broke into the fire. Fortunately, the MiG pilots weren't sharpshooters, and their cannon had a very slow rate of fire. It didn't last as long as it seemed, but those four MiGs made me work from 20,000 ft all the way down to the deck to shake them.

'During some of the violent manoeuvring, I warped my wings to the point that they had to be replaced. I don't know why all four of them came after me and left Gibson alone, but it didn't take long for my fear to turn into rage. At one point, when I had one of them in my sights, I burned out the barrels because the rounds were tumbling ineffectively toward the MiG I was firing at.

'We were far north, close to the river, and I was very low on fuel, but at least I had kept Capt Gibson's tail clear during the fight. I had to shut the engine down and glide home from 45,000 ft. When I was close enough to enter the pattern, I restarted and landed without incident long after the others. They'd already written me off, so they were glad to see me. What a day it had been. I'd landed with less than ten gallons of fuel in my internal tanks.'

Another young pilot to experience life as a wingman was 1Lt Richard F Merian of the 335th FS;

'I had several missions under my belt before I ever saw my first MiG. I was participating in a group-strength mission, with two squadrons strung out at different altitudes. A very large battle developed into what looked like a swarm of bees, with everyone trying to line up on everyone else. The leader of my flight was a guy from wing HQ. I hadn't flown with him before. He just kind of cruised through the whole fight without firing his guns. It was an interesting experience flying No 4 in a flight of four. I knew what to expect when flying as a wingman for many of the experienced guys in my squadron, but when your wing leaders came down from 4th FW HQ, you didn't know much about them.

'Fortunately, I was able to fly wing for some of the great ones – John Meyer, Billy Hovde, Glenn Eagleston and "Gabby" Gabreski to name but a few. I remember one time I was flying wing for Col Eagleston and we were by ourselves. Before I knew it, we had ten MiG-15s cornered between us and home. We fought our way out, but not before the colonel had relaxed me by radioing, "if you're scared, then so am I".'

Like many of his contemporaries, 2Lt John Ridout of the 334th FS was fresh out of flight school when he received a plum posting to the 4th FW in the Far East. Unfortunately, he was seriously hurt in a landing accident

1Lt Ralph 'Hoot' Gibson became the USAF's third jet ace while flying with the 335th FS, claiming his fifth kill on 9 September 1951. Just 23 minutes earlier, 334th FS pilot 1Lt Richard Becker had downed his fifth MiG-15 to become the second Sabre ace of the conflict (*Leo Fournier*)

Col Francis Gabreski (right) congratulates 1Lts Richard Becker (left) and Ralph Gibson (centre) on their 'ace-making' kills shortly after their 9 September missions. The 28-victory Thunderbolt ace of World War 2 had himself bagged his second of an eventual 6.5 MiGs exactly one week earlier. Assigned to the 4th FW HQ at the time, Gabreski would duly become the eighth Sabre ace whilst leading the 51st FW in April 1952 (*Richard Becker*)

which cut short his combat tour at 54 missions. Frustratingly for Ridout, he had just qualified as an element lead when he suffered his injuries, which meant that he flew just ten missions as a 'shooter'. His tour recollections give a detailed insight into life with a frontline Sabre squadron at Kimpo in 1951;

'Our primary mission was to provide a protective screen for our fighter-bombers when they attacked targets deep in North Korea, blocking any attempt made by the MiG-15s to interfere with their mission. At this particular time in the war, they rarely engaged the Sabres, except to get past us for a quick shot at the F-84s and F-80s, before zooming back up to altitude. With notable individual exceptions, the average skill level of the MiG pilots was substantially inferior to that of their American counterparts. They were not using cohesive team tactics, and they seemed significantly deficient in instrument flying skills. This conclusion was based upon their marked reluctance to enter clouds, even when under close attack by F-86s. This was probably because their jets lacked adequate instrumentation, or the pilots had not been effectively trained in blind flying techniques.

'Our normal routine was to initiate withdrawal when our fuel gauges showed we had about 1200 pounds remaining, which meant that we could safely return to Kimpo AB for a power-on landing approach, with a modest reserve for contingencies. However, things became rather uncomfortable if you found yourself at this fuel level with MiGs coming up to engage! We were regularly faced with just such a situation because the enemy knew precisely when an F-86 combat patrol was close to hitting "bingo" fuel.

'In such cases, Sabre pilots became overly aggressive, hoping to quickly fend off the MiGs with a brief and violent encounter. If everything went to plan, several minutes later they would have the opportunity to break away from the communist fighters, but occasionally pilots did not have enough fuel to reach base. A few jets were duly lost due to fuel starvation, while others gained altitude quickly and were able to dead stick land back at Kimpo.'

NIGHTFLYING

Although the Sabre was never used as a nightfighter in Korea due to it lacking a radar, there were occasions when aircraft landed back at Kimpo with little or no daylight left. Such landings were very hazardous due to poor runway lighting, and were usually undertaken by pilots who had just completed a universally hated last light reconnaissance sweep. 1Lt Ridout recalled;

'These late missions involved sending two or four F-86s up to "MiG Alley" just before dark to look at the activity at the enemy air bases north of the Yalu River. From the

Although communist infiltrators rarely attempted to gain access to the major air bases in South Korea, the security forces never decreased their vigilance. With a Sabre flightline providing a hugely attractive target, dozens of guards such as this one, patrolling with his German Shepherd, would be kept busy making the rounds late at night while the 4th FW's pilots slept in their quarters (*Bill Graski*)

In June 1951, famous radio news commentator H V Kaltenborn visited Kimpo AB expressly to meet the 4th FW. Amongst the pilots that he conversed with were future aces 1Lt Richard Becker (left) and 1Lt Ralph 'Hoot' Gibson (right) (*Richard Becker*)

information we gathered, our Intelligence types tried to estimate the level of enemy air activity that would be likely the next day. It was a very lonesome feeling to be 200 miles from home base, knowing that you had a limited fuel supply, and that the enemy knew exactly what your remaining time was before you had to head south. You knew that at this point, the MiGs would probably show up. The communists had a very good GCI (ground-control intercept) set-up, and that gave them a distinct advantage at all times, especially if it was overcast with scattered clouds.'

Enemy formation strengths and tactics continued to vary widely during the summer of 1951, and USAF Intelligence officers struggled to get a grip on exactly what the MiG units were doing, or what they were ultimately trying to achieve, as a result.

At the time, the UN still believed that all MiG-15s in-theatre were manned by either North Korean or Chinese pilots. In fact, Soviet units were being regularly rotated through the Antung Complex, and FEAF Intelligence only began to pick up that regiments were being swapped when it started to document the various markings and colours worn on the MiGs that were being engaged over the Yalu. Such information was gleaned during formal debriefings with pilots recently returned from 'MiG Alley', when the action that they had fought was still fresh in their minds.

Although some knowledge of MiG units was built up this way, the FEAF remained oblivious to the fact that a significant number of these aircraft were being flown by Soviet pilots until well after the war had ended.

Amongst the units identified through their markings, one in particular seemed to get more than its share of publicity within the Sabre ranks in 1951. The regiment flew MiG-15s that were painted powder blue overall, as opposed to the majority of communist jet fighters that were encountered, which were in the main unpainted, bar their red stars, 'Bort' number and occasional nose flash. The powder blue jets appeared periodically during the last two years of the war, and their pilots displayed superb airmanship.

2Lt Ridout encountered this elite regiment during one of his early patrols over the Yalu River;

'On this particular mission, I was flying wing for our flight leader, Capt Jere Lewis. We were cruising along the south bank of the Yalu at the point right below the big MiG base at Antung. We were at about 20,000 ft, and could easily see a large number of enemy fighters lined up in the parking areas. There was a heavy cloud deck about 500 ft above us, which was just enough to keep the MiGs from dropping down on our "six o'clock". I remember thinking that the setting sun, reflecting off the dark water, clouds and anti-aircraft bursts was one of the most intriguing sights that I had ever seen!

'Suddenly, we were shocked to find four MiG-15s coming out of the cloud layer right onto our "six o'clock". Obviously, they had some very good GCI support, and these pilots could handle the instrument flying to perfection! The lead MiG pilot fired one burst at us, but fortunately the rate of fire on his cannon was rather slow and we flew through it without taking any hits. Actually, we flew right through some flaming golf balls, or it seemed like it. With the spacing between the rounds, we had a gap to get through unscathed.

'Immediately after that first burst things got interesting, and we ended up in a very tight circle to the right, swapping altitude for air speed. This was a basic Lufbery Circle manoeuvre, with me slightly inside of Capt Lewis's turn and the MiGs strung out in trail behind us. This is a nice safe manoeuvre, because no one can get enough lead for a deflection shot until the decreasing altitude forces someone to roll out. Then things start to get tough!

'This situation gave us a slight advantage, and Lewis was beginning to achieve position to start firing on their No 4 man. At that point, No 4 reversed his turn, which made him a sitting duck for our leader if he had chosen to follow him, but experience counts in these situations! We later decided that the MiG leader had ordered the roll out to bait us into giving him an equally clear shot, at the possible expense of his own No 4!

'All of a sudden I heard a loud bang right behind the cockpit, and I thought I had taken a hit, but it was just the APU (auxiliary power unit) access door popping open. The G-meter was giving rather high readings, but at that moment in time I was not overly concerned! Lewis played the diving turn beautifully to get us transonic, and at that speed and altitude, we had better flight controls than the MiG. Low fuel made further engagement suicidal, so we used our speed to exit the fight. Those guys were aggressive and well trained, and they still had some fight left in them when we departed.'

2Lt Ridout's flight back to Kimpo was uneventful, but the debriefing proved to be quite the opposite. The Intelligence people were very interested in the communist pilots' change of tactics, and the fact that all of the MiGs encountered were powder blue in colour. It had been some months since this elite unit had crossed swords with the Sabres, and their colour scheme made the jets very difficult to see in clouds or hazy conditions. Several days after Ridout's debriefing, it was confirmed that he and his section leader had run into a crack East German all-weather unit. Post-war, the USAF discovered that most Warsaw Pact countries had sent MiG-15 regiments into Manchuria in order to gain valuable experience fighting F-86s.

All Sabre units that saw action in the Korean War encountered the powder blue MiGs at one time or another, as well as camouflaged jets and more common all-silver fighters with red noses or solid red vertical stabilisers. 1Lt Willard P 'Bill' Dunbar, who flew a full combat tour with the 336th FS, recalled some of the different schemes that he faced over northwest Korea;

'There were several different paint jobs that appeared from time to time on the MiGs that we fought during my tour. Some were powder blue, but

most were just all-silver, with big red stars. Toward the latter part of my tour with the 4th, I saw several MiGs that were painted in a solid Hawthorne Green scheme, as well as a few with bright yellow markings. It slowly became evident to all of us that we were facing a large number of different units drawn from all over the Soviet bloc. We always suspected that some of the MiGs we fought were flown by Russians – especially those that were piloted by "honchos", who clearly knew their stuff.

'Proof of this came during a sortie that I flew as wingman to ace Capt Robinson "Robbie" Risner, who claimed one of his eight kills during the course of the mission. An extraordinary pilot, Risner, having shot the canopy off his MiG, ran right up alongside the stricken aircraft. The communist pilot was still sat in the cockpit of his jet, but he was minus his helmet – this had probably blown off in the slipstream soon after the canopy had been shot away. Despite his predicament, the pilot, who had red hair and a very light complexion, was shaking his fist at Robbie. No oriental, he suddenly made a fast break for the airfield at Antung at about 0.9 Mach. We watched from a distance as the MiG landed way too fast and rolled up in a ball of dirt and dust about a mile off the other end of the runway.'

One could write a book detailing the many different tactics that the MiG pilots used against the F-86s and the more vulnerable UN fighter-bombers. Most of these were countered quickly by the experienced flight leaders, but occasionally some manoeuvres worked for a day or so – especially the ones that involved high-speed, diving passes, followed by zooming climbs back up to altitude.

A perennial favourite amongst all MiG pilots was the 'sucker' tactic known as 'The Decoy'. Many of the less experienced Sabre pilots that were overly hungry for a kill had a tendency to go after any lone MiGs that they spotted, but usually their experienced section leads intervened. 1Lt Dunbar's first-hand experience of this ploy resulted in his fighter being fired at for the very first time;

'There was a single MiG way out in front of five others that were trailing at a much lower altitude. This was a good manoeuvre on their part, because once an F-86 had fallen in behind the loner and was preparing to fire, one or more of the MiGs would zoom up from below and fire at the Sabre from underneath. With the weight differential very much in favour of the MiG-15, this manoeuvre took very little effort to perform. If the pilot was an experienced shooter, his firepower could blast a Sabre out of the sky before the pilot in the latter jet even knew that he was under attack.

'Once our Intelligence folks learned more about the MiG's flight characteristics, it became clear why it was to the communist pilots' advantage to come up from below, as opposed to performing a high speed

F-86E-10 51-2824 of the 336th FS was one of the highest-scoring aircraft in the 4th FW prior to its demise in combat on 20 July 1953. Nicknamed *Ohio Mike/Little Mike*, the jet was assigned to the 4th FW in late 1951 and carried 13 victory symbols for kills credited to several pilots. Most of these had been claimed by the 336th FS's ranking ace, Maj Robinson Risner, although at least one was scored by fellow ace Maj Stephen Bettinger (see page 78). Indeed, the latter was forced to eject from 51-2824 just minutes later after the fighter had been badly shot up by another MiG (*Ernie Atkinson*)

1Lt Bill Dunbar flew as wingman for numerous 336th FS pilots in 1952, including ace Maj Robinson Risner (*USAF*)

dive from above. There were just too many dive restrictions on the MiG, and some of them came apart when they headed straight down with an F-86 on their tail. If we had had better knowledge of why they were using certain tactics, we would have achieved more kills and suffered fewer losses. Knowledge about the MiG improved as the war went on, and the pilots that followed after I left in the autumn of 1952 got better Intel briefings due to the combat experience we had gained.'

B-29 Escort

Although the previously mentioned 'last light' reconnaissance sorties were never relished by Sabre pilots, in 1951 the 4th FW was briefly tasked with flying another mission which proved to be every bit as difficult unpopular – escorting big, slow B-29 Superfortresses bombing key targets on the Yalu River in daylight.

On many of these missions, it was hard to form a barrier patrol between the MiG bases and the bombers if the latter were in a box formation directly above the river. To the north of the waterway was Manchuria, over which the Sabres were strictly forbidden from flying. This meant that the F-86 pilots had very little room for manoeuvre in their attempts to defend the B-29s from the swarms of MiG-15s based north of the Yalu.

The heavy bombers had already levelled North Korea's industrial base prior to the MiG-15's appearance, but with the entry of China into the war in late November 1950, the number of targets multiplied when enormous stockpiles of supplies for the invading Peoples' Army appeared just south of the Yalu. These huge storage centres had to be hit, not only by the fighter-bombers but the B-29s too.

The USAF persevered with daylight bombing raids well into October 1951, when losses to aggressive MiGs proved too costly to bear. Many former Soviet pilots who went up against the B-29s stated that the slow-moving 'heavies' were their targets of choice because the bombers' had the ability to inflict major damage on the communist war effort. The presence of F-86s offered the bomber crews a modicum of protection, although on many occasions all the Sabre pilots managed to do was to provoke more determined attacks from the MiG pilots. The latter could easily hit and run from their higher attacking altitudes, and the F-86 pilots had very little chance to respond to these slashing runs unless they in turn chased the enemy fighters deeper into Manchuria.

Conversely, when the bombers struck targets further south within 'MiG Alley', the Sabre units were able to maintain an effective escort-ing position, resulting in the MiGs paying a much higher price for their successes.

The impact of the relentless MiG

The 4th FW's F-86s primarily flew two types of missions in Korea – combat air patrols over enemy territory, where the pilots went looking for MiGs, and fighter escort for medium and heavy bombers, as well as fighter-bombers. The latter held much more responsibility, and required a lot of coordination and pre-planning. Here, 1Lt Richard Becker (second from the right) is briefed along with other pilots in his flight for a mission involving three flights of four 334th FS F-86As. The pilot to Becker's right is 2Lt Andy Anderson, who was rated as one of the best wingmen in the 4th FW by 335th FS CO Maj Philip Van Sickle (*Richard Becker*)

Group CO Col Ben Preston holds up a freshly-painted sign which gives details of the success that his unit had enjoyed on 16 October 1951 – nine MiGs confirmed destroyed and six damaged. This was one of the 4th's best single-day hauls up to this point in the war, with Preston leading by example with a MiG kill. HQ staff pilot Maj Frank Fisher, standing third from left, doubled his CO's tally on the day, and was also credited with having damaged a third MiG. Fisher came tantalisingly close to 'acedom', finishing his tour with four kills, one probable and two damaged to his credit. He was one of 13 Sabre pilots to claim four kills with the 4th FW in Korea (*USAF*)

attacks against the B-29s reached a fever pitch in September and October 1951.

September also proved to be a pivotal month for UN fighter-bombers too, as they came under sustained attack from communist fighters. The latter were swarming all over northern Korea in such large numbers that they were breaking through the Sabre screen and either shooting down a handful of fighter-bombers at a time, or making entire formations salvo their bombs prematurely in order to defend themselves against attack. Either way, the MiG pilots were achieving their objective.

Documents from this period state that 4th FW pilots reported no fewer than 911 communist aircraft sightings/contacts during September, which far exceeded the figures for previous months. By late October things were getting out of hand for the 4th FW, which was struggling to prevent the MiGs from getting through. Indeed, things got so bad that the FEAF declared that daylight bomber losses were unacceptable and duly switched to night missions.

The communist fighters' increased operational tempo was triggered, in part, by bombing raids on three North Korean airfields at Saamcham, Taechon and Namsi that were then under construction. Events came to a head on 23 October, which was subsequently dubbed 'Black Tuesday', when three of the eight 307th BG B-29s sortied from Kadena AB, Okinawa, to bomb Namsi were shot down by possibly as many as 150 MiGs. A further four Superfortresses were badly damaged when the group's F-84 escorts were totally overwhelmed.

One final daylight raid was made on 28 October, before USAF chief of staff Gen Hoyt S Vandenberg stepped in and ordered a stop to these missions.

During the month of October the FEAF had lost seven F-86s, five B-29s, two F-84s and an RF-80 in combat, with most of these falling to MiGs (the latter claimed five of the Sabres). In return, the 4th FW was credited with 25 kills, which was its highest monthly tally to date. By comparison, 12 MiGs had been downed the previous month for six F-86s lost on operations, half of the latter falling to communist jets.

It was these losses to the ever-growing ranks of MiG-15s north of the Yalu River that finally resulted in the USAF transferring new F-86Es to the Far East and Korea ahead of schedule. The 4th FW simply had insufficient resources in-theatre to retain daylight aerial supremacy and provide fighter protection for the numerous bomber and fighter-bomber missions that were taking place on a daily basis over North Korea.

As a direct result of the problems facing the 4th, in late October the FEAF was forced to restrict virtually all B-29 missions to the hours of darkness, and seriously curtail unescorted deep fighter-bomber penetrations into northwest Korea until the winter months had passed.

When a Sabre returned from a mission to Kimpo AB with its hydraulics shot out, the emergency safety barrier seen here would be raised at the end of the runway to prevent the pilot and his jet from running off into the sand and dirt. The two F-86s shown here, both fitted with full external tanks, are destined for 'MiG Alley' (*Bill Graski*)

Targets for the latter missions were just too close to the MiG bases in Manchuria.

4th FW HQ pilot Maj Franklin L Fisher claimed two of his three MiG kills whilst escorting B-29s during October 1951. He remembered;

'On the mission that comes to mind, we put up 32 Sabres (a combination of 334th and 336th FS aircraft) to rendezvous with a formation of 12 bombers that were coming in from Kadena AB. This was a well coordinated plan, with flak suppression provided by F-51 Mustangs down at tree-top level 30 minutes before the B-29s arrived in the area. All of the targets this far north were well defended by anti-aircraft artillery emplacements.

'The bombers were in "boxes" of three each following in trail. We were in four-ship flights, with 16 Sabres flying directly over the bombers at 0.86 mach. We were forced to fly "S" turns at 25,000 ft in order to maintain position over the slower aircraft.

'The other 16 Sabres on the mission set up a screen to the north, ahead of the bombers. After the B-29s had joined up over Hamhung, all mission aircraft switched from rendezvous radio channel to combat common channel. Immediately after dropping their ordnance, the bombers turned left 150 degrees, which pointed them back in the direction of Kadena. Our fighter screen took a position of close escort over the last bomber formation.

'Everything was quiet, and we watched our fuel level gradually move down to "bingo". By this time we were well out of the MiGs' range, so it was time to release the bombers and head back south. The sky was clear and visibility was unlimited. This mission had been flown on one of those rare days in October when the MiGs chose not to come up and challenge us, or the B-29s. If they had, we would have been in position to take them on' "

The Russian pilots, and their Warsaw Pact brethren, were very well versed in defensive tactics, as that was their sole mission when back in Europe. Defending 'Mother Russia' had priority over any offensive operations, and the MiG series of aircraft were designed for high speed, high altitude intercepts.

Boasting only a modest range, the jets were restricted to limited distance operations over 'MiG Alley', where pilots worked well with their GCI operators. The latter was not required, however, when it came to intercepting large heavy bomber formations in clear weather during daylight. And although switching to night missions reduced B-29 losses, the bombers were now sought out by all-weather/night-qualified MiG pilots who had little problem locating the bomber streams with the help of GCI. The communist pilots became so proficient at night intercepts that a number of F-84 Thunderjets flying nocturnal missions also disappeared without a trace over North Korea.

SABRE BOMBER KILLS

Although pilots from the 4th FW spent the vast majority of their time tangling with MiG-15s, very occasionally other communist aircraft would be encountered over North Korea. USAF Intelligence knew that the NKPAF included a significant number of Tupolev Tu-2 twin-engined bombers within its ranks, and these theoretically posed a real threat to the frontline troops. However, the constant F-86 patrols seemed to deter their widespread use. Even so, at least nine Tu-2 kills were attributed to F-86 pilots, and most of these were downed on 30 November 1951, when 31 Sabres encountered 12 of the bombers, escorted by 16 La-9s and 18 MiG-15s. One of the pilots involved in the interception was Capt Raymond O Barton of the 334th FS;

'My second kill of the war wasn't a MiG but a Tu-2 bomber, equipped with "stingers" in the tail – two 20 mm cannon. We heard they were coming, and encountered them heading south right off the coast of North Korea. I set up for the classic training solution of a turn reversing gunnery curve, but quickly dumped the idea. Instead, I broke left and came back around. This time, I stuck my nose right up the bomber's tail, squeezed off a long burst and it blew up.

'I flew right through the debris, and from the size of the explosion, I think his bombs blew up. I broke left again and was going to make another pass when I checked my "six o'clock" to clear for my wingman. All of a sudden the SOB started shooting at me, and only then did I realise it was a MiG and not my wingman! It was at this time that I discovered I'd attracted far more than one MiG. I turned into them and kind of bluffed my way out of the first gaggle and tried to call my wingman, but got no answer. So I turned back north to see if I could spot a 'chute or a raft or something, but no joy.

'Now the MiGs were all around me, and I developed a technique of trying to run them out of ammo! I called for help, and the only response I got was from my roommate, Maj George Davis. I'll never forget his reply. "I don't have enough fuel left either but I'm on the way". All the MiGs except one had left the area. I had a huge hole where my left fuel cap had been, but I was still flying. When George reached me, he asked me to make a couple of identifying turn reversals. I reluctantly did, and he shot that SOB right off my butt. We made it home, where I found out my wingman had made it back okay. He'd gone after one of the Tu-2s and we got separated. He latched on to another F-86 for the flight back to Kimpo. My jet was repaired with a new fuel bladder and a filler cap. Amazingly, there was no structural damage.'

Maj Davis was credited with three Tu-2s and one MiG-15 destroyed following the mission, which combined with two MiG kills on 27 November to make him the fifth ace of the conflict. Davis would ultimately boost his tally to 14 victories prior to being killed in action on 10 February 1952.

These Tu-2s had been shot down by pilots flying new E-model F-86s, which had started arriving in Korea in early October 1951. Overseeing the introduction of the new variant into service with the 4th FW was one

World War 2 fighter ace, and 334th FS CO, Maj George Davis poses for one of the most enduring images to come out of the Korean War. This photograph was taken soon after he had become the USAF's fifth Sabre ace on 30 November 1951 (*USAF*)

of North American's most experienced and knowledgeable 'tech reps', Pennock 'Penny' Bowen, who commented to the press at the time on the rugged nature of the Sabre, and how well designed it was to absorb punishment;

'The battle damage that the F-86 can take and still come back safely to base, is phenomenal! Although it isn't subjected to heavy anti-aircraft fire and the stresses of low altitude flying, it still has to face the large-calibre cannon that the MiG-15 has. It has already been proven in combat that the Sabre will fly perfectly well with only one operable aileron, flap and elevator, and with gaping holes in its wings.

It very seldom took more than one or two hits from a MiG-15's powerful 37 mm cannon to bring down an aircraft. This pilot stands alongside the severe damage done to the flaps on the left wing of his 4th FW Sabre following an altercation with a MiG. If the round had hit the wing root itself, the wing might have separated from the fuselage (*John Henderson*)

'During my early weeks at Kimpo AB (where the 4th FW started receiving a few of the new E-models), I had the opportunity of examining battle damage to aircraft of other manufacturers. This also included my conversing with many pilots who had had the opportunity of comparing the damage received by F-86s to the damage received by other types under similar circumstances. Most agree that the Sabre can withstand the most punishment. Moreover, pilots have constantly praised the handling characteristics of it after it had sustained severe battle damage. During intense combat situations (dogfights), red lines are frequently disregarded and aircraft limitations constantly exceeded. I can recall several cases where 10 Gs were imposed on the Sabre, and with only one exception, the jets all eventually flew regular missions again.'

The work ethic and skill of the 4th FW's maintenance personnel in Korea also came in for praise from 'Penny' Bowen;

'The efficiency of the groundcrews of the 4th FW was unbelievable. There were several times when we had an F-86 on the ground because one

Two pilots from the 335th FS walk out to their jets prior to flying an early-morning patrol 'up north'. They would have risen before dawn to attend a briefing, and to check out their survival gear. The squadron's parking area at Kimpo AB was covered in PSP (*Bill Graski*)

wing was badly shot up from enemy action and spare wings were not available. In subsequent aerial battles during which an F-86 received a wing hit, the pilot would report the damage, and which wing was hit, on the radio as he returned to base. If the hit was taken in a wing opposite from the damaged wing of a grounded fighter, the mechanics would meet the returning aircraft and start removing the good wing as soon as the engine was shut down. Within 30 hours the grounded F-86 would be flying combat missions once again!'

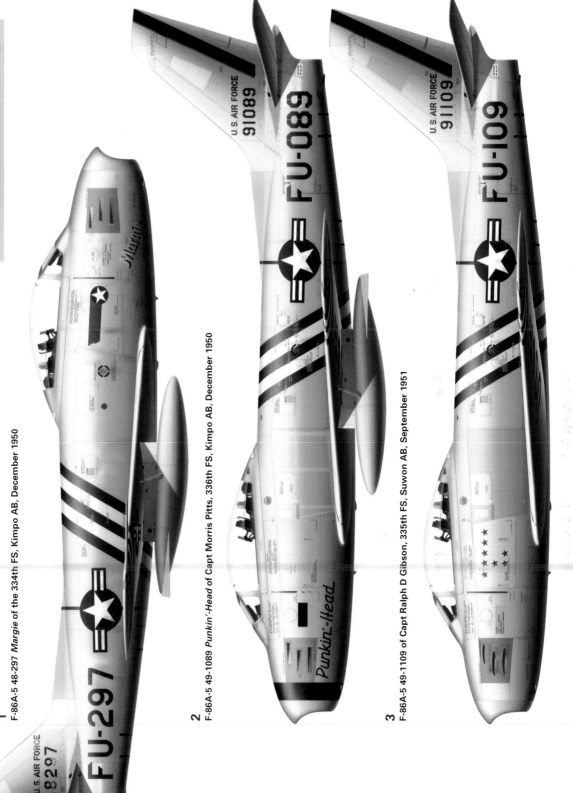

1
F-86A-5 48-297 *Margie* of the 334th FS, Kimpo AB, December 1950

2
F-86A-5 49-1089 *Punkin'-Head* of Capt Morris Pitts, 336th FS, Kimpo AB, December 1950

3
F-86A-5 49-1109 of Capt Ralph D Gibson, 335th FS, Suwon AB, September 1951

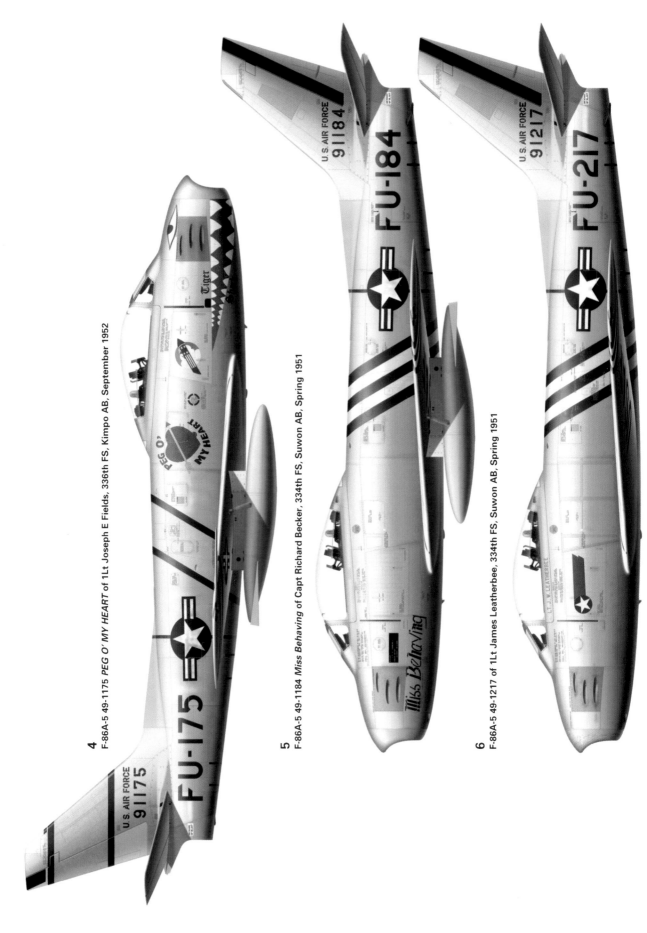

4

F-86A-5 49-1175 *PEG O' MY HEART* of 1Lt Joseph E Fields, 336th FS, Kimpo AB, September 1952

5

F-86A-5 49-1184 *Miss Behaving* of Capt Richard Becker, 334th FS, Suwon AB, Spring 1951

6

F-86A-5 49-1217 of 1Lt James Leatherbee, 334th FS, Suwon AB, Spring 1951

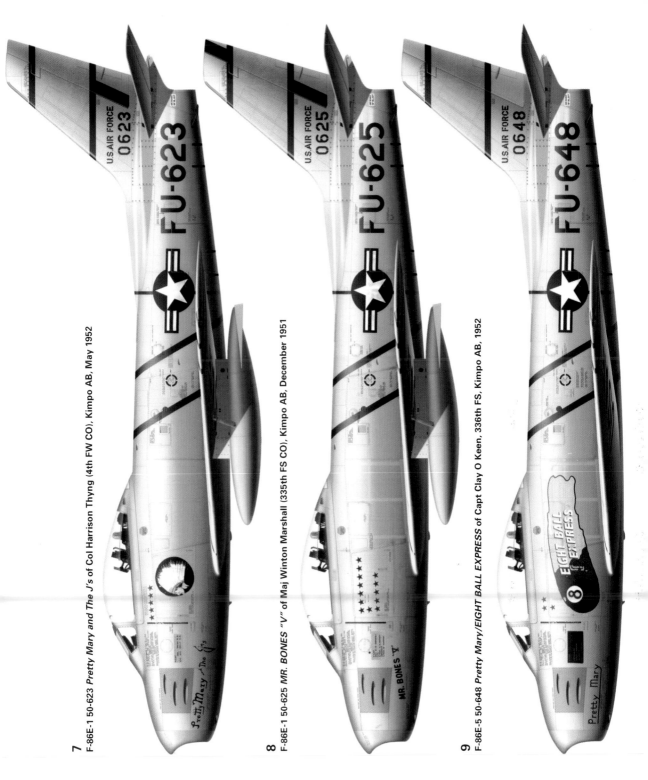

7
F-86E-1 50-623 *Pretty Mary and The J's* of Col Harrison Thyng (4th FW CO), Kimpo AB, May 1952

8
F-86E-1 50-625 *MR. BONES "V"* of Maj Winton Marshall (335th FS CO), Kimpo AB, December 1951

9
F-86E-5 50-648 *Pretty Mary/EIGHT BALL EXPRESS* of Capt Clay O Keen, 336th FS, Kimpo AB, 1952

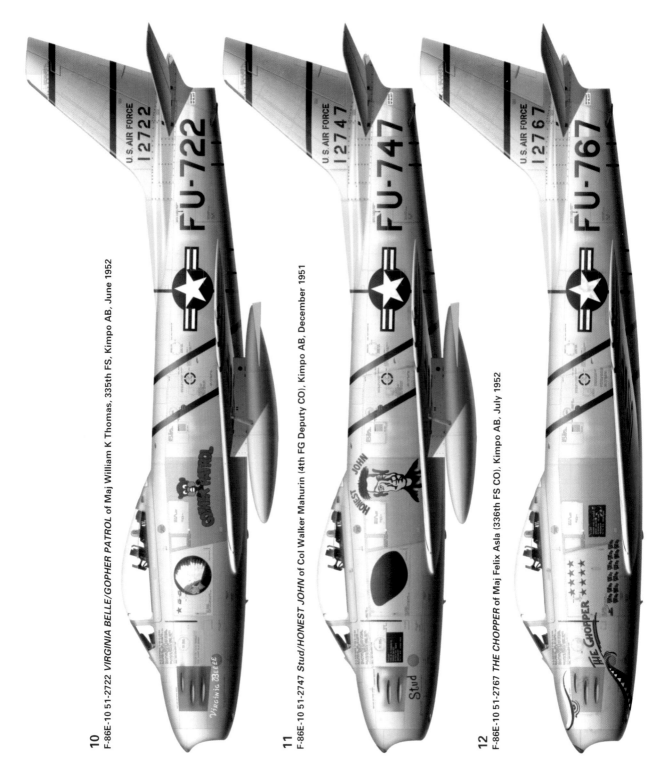

10
F-86E-10 51-2722 *VIRGINIA BELLE/GOPHER PATROL* of Maj William K Thomas, 335th FS, Kimpo AB, June 1952

11
F-86E-10 51-2747 *Stud/HONEST JOHN* of Col Walker Mahurin (4th FG Deputy CO), Kimpo AB, December 1951

12
F-86E-10 51-2767 *THE CHOPPER* of Maj Felix Asla (336th FS CO), Kimpo AB, July 1952

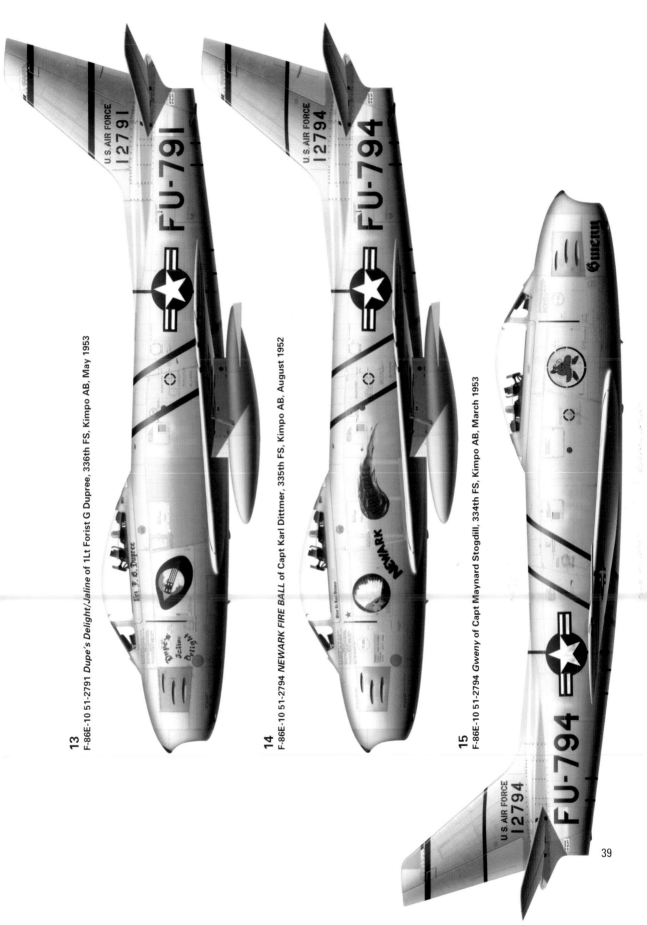

13
F-86E-10 51-2791 *Dupe's Delight/Jaline* of 1Lt Forist G Dupree, 336th FS, Kimpo AB, May 1953

14
F-86E-10 51-2794 *NEWARK FIRE BALL* of Capt Karl Dittmer, 335th FS, Kimpo AB, August 1952

15
F-86E-10 51-2794 *Gweny* of Capt Maynard Stogdill, 334th FS, Kimpo AB, March 1953

39

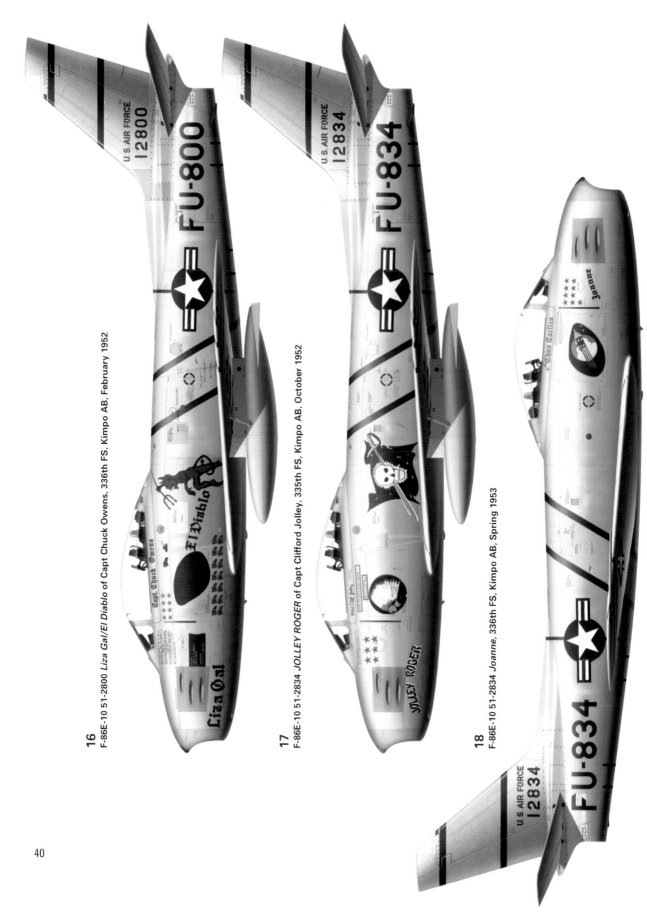

16
F-86E-10 51-2800 *Liza Gal/El Diablo* of Capt Chuck Owens, 336th FS, Kimpo AB, February 1952

17
F-86E-10 51-2834 *JOLLEY ROGER* of Capt Clifford Jolley, 335th FS, Kimpo AB, October 1952

18
F-86E-10 51-2834 *Joanne*, 336th FS, Kimpo AB, Spring 1953

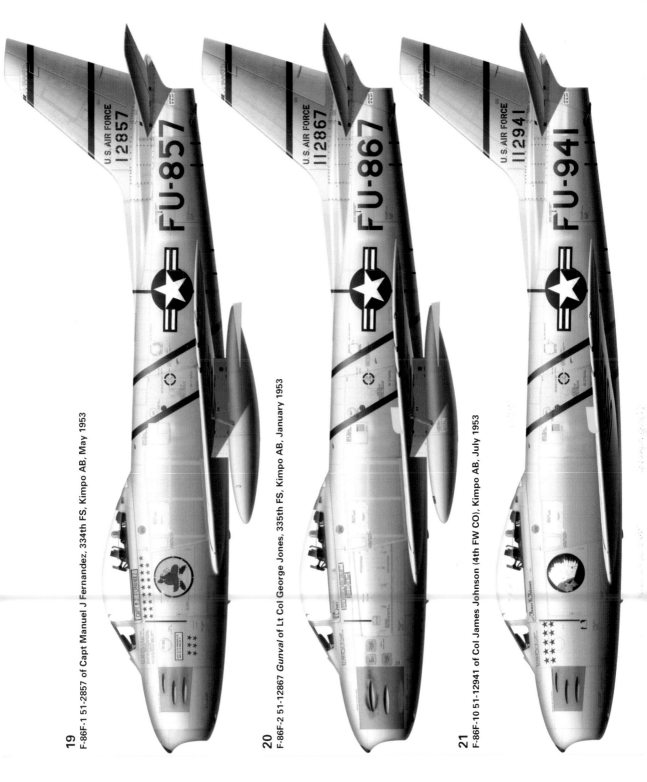

19
F-86F-1 51-2857 of Capt Manuel J Fernandez, 334th FS, Kimpo AB, May 1953

20
F-86F-2 51-12867 *Gunval* of Lt Col George Jones, 335th FS, Kimpo AB, January 1953

21
F-86F-10 51-12941 of Col James Johnson (4th FW CO), Kimpo AB, July 1953

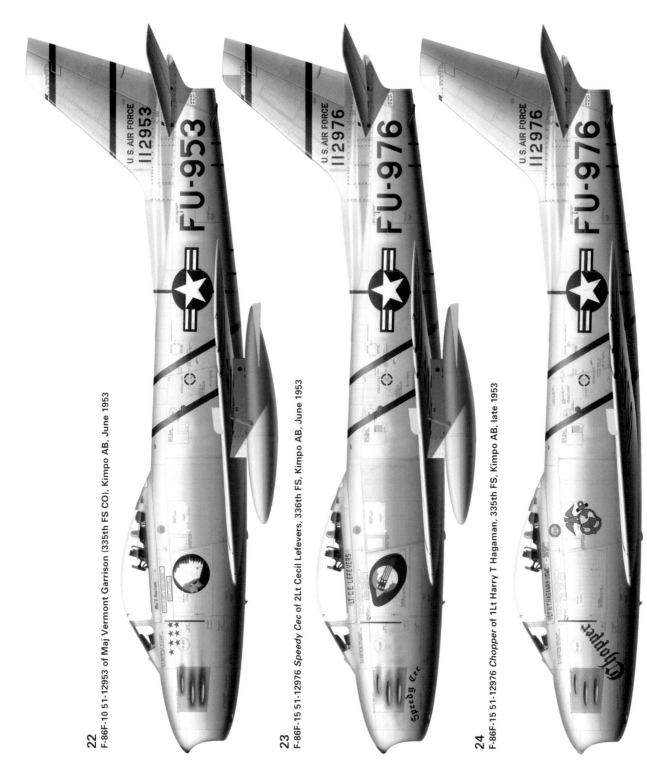

22
F-86F-10 51-12953 of Maj Vermont Garrison (335th FS CO), Kimpo AB, June 1953

23
F-86F-15 51-12976 *Speedy Cec* of 2Lt Cecil Lefevers, 336th FS, Kimpo AB, June 1953

24
F-86F-15 51-12976 *Chopper* of 1Lt Harry T Hagaman, 335th FS, Kimpo AB, late 1953

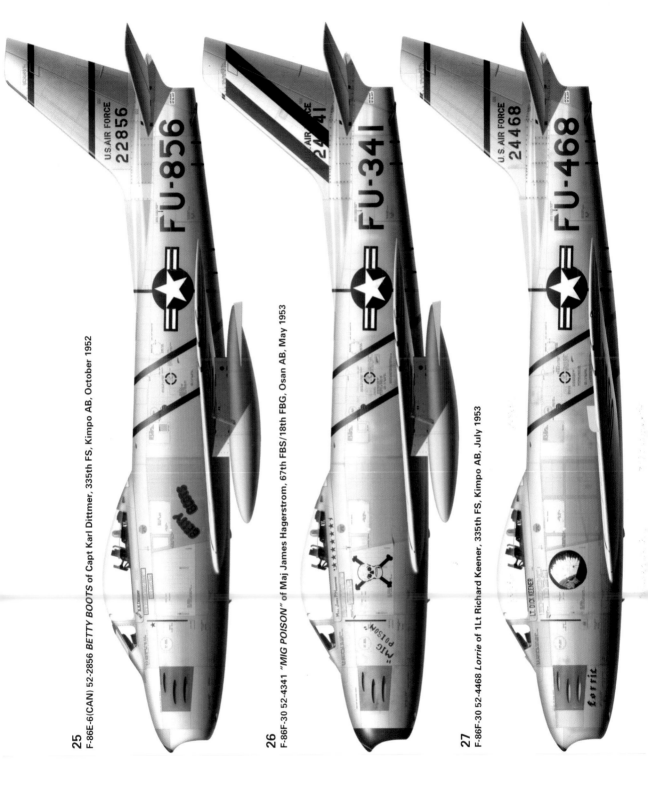

25
F-86E-6(CAN) 52-2856 *BETTY BOOTS* of Capt Karl Dittmer, 335th FS, Kimpo AB, October 1952

26
F-86F-30 52-4341 *"MIG POISON"* of Maj James Hagerstrom, 67th FBS/18th FBG, Osan AB, May 1953

27
F-86F-30 52-4468 *Lorrie* of 1Lt Richard Keener, 335th FS, Kimpo AB, July 1953

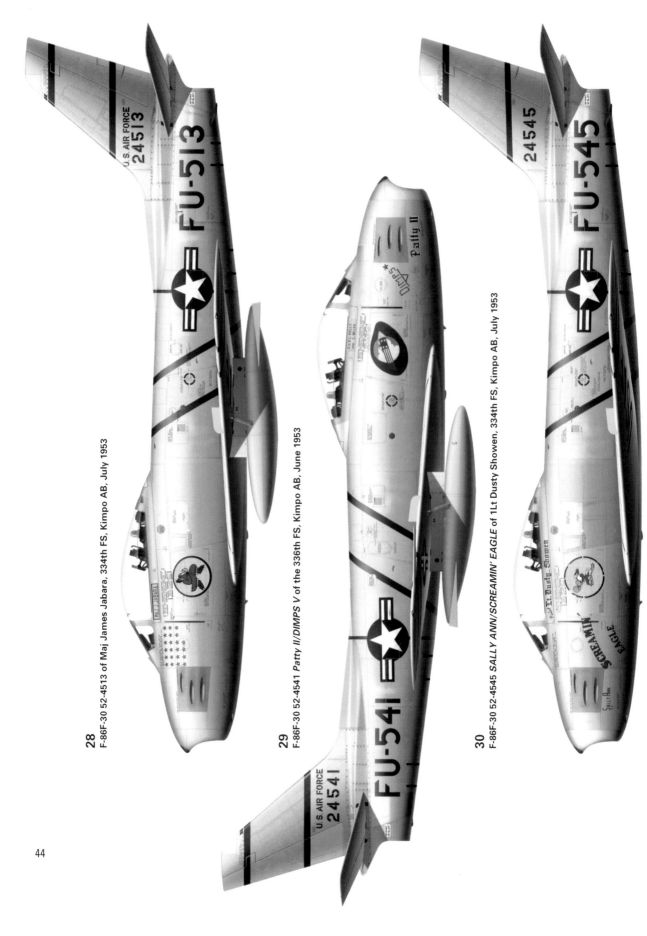

28
F-86F-30 52-4513 of Maj James Jabara, 334th FS, Kimpo AB, July 1953

29
F-86F-30 52-4541 *Patty II/DIMPS V* of the 336th FS, Kimpo AB, June 1953

30
F-86F-30 52-4545 *SALLY ANN/SCREAMIN' EAGLE* of 1Lt Dusty Showen, 334th FS, Kimpo AB, July 1953

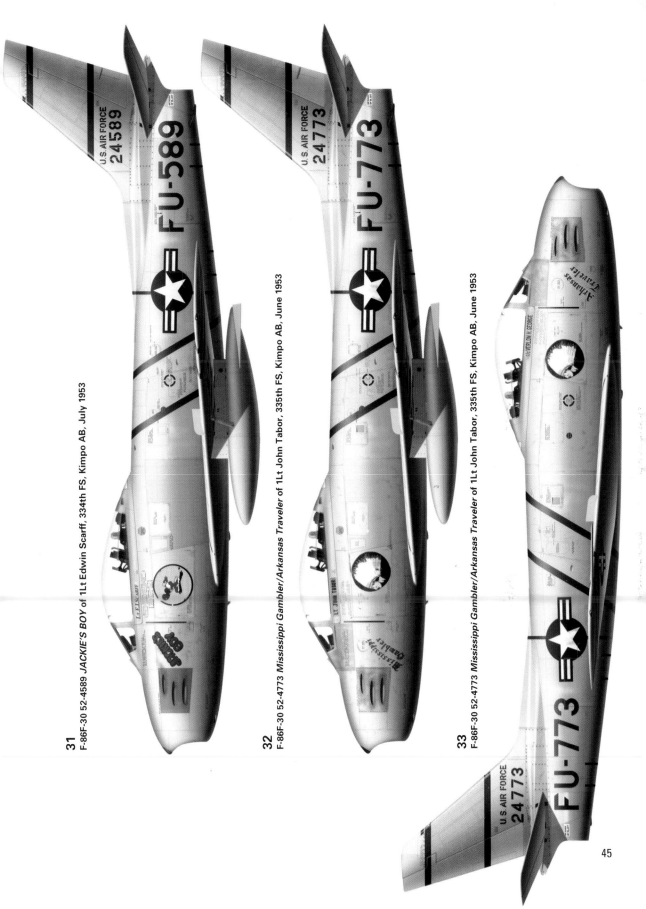

31
F-86F-30 52-4589 *JACKIE'S BOY* of 1Lt Edwin Scarff, 334th FS, Kimpo AB, July 1953

32
F-86F-30 52-4773 *Mississippi Gambler/Arkansas Traveler* of 1Lt John Tabor, 335th FS, Kimpo AB, June 1953

33
F-86F-30 52-4773 *Mississippi Gambler/Arkansas Traveler* of 1Lt John Tabor, 335th FS, Kimpo AB, June 1953

45

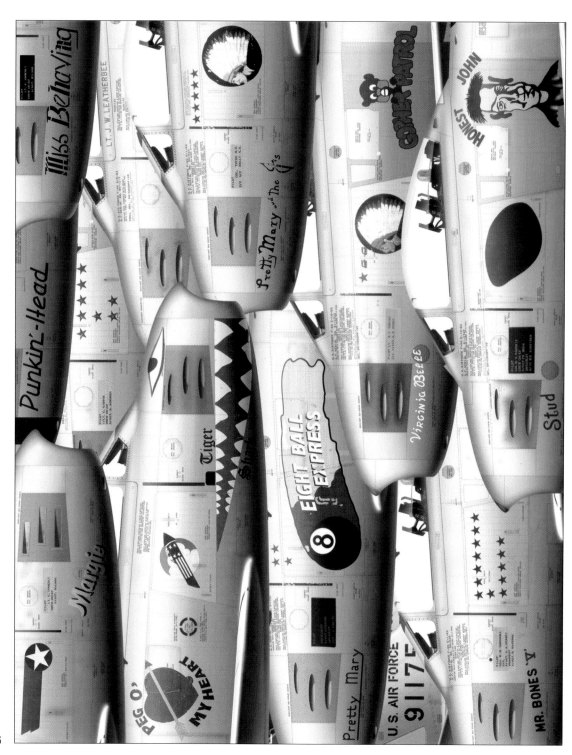

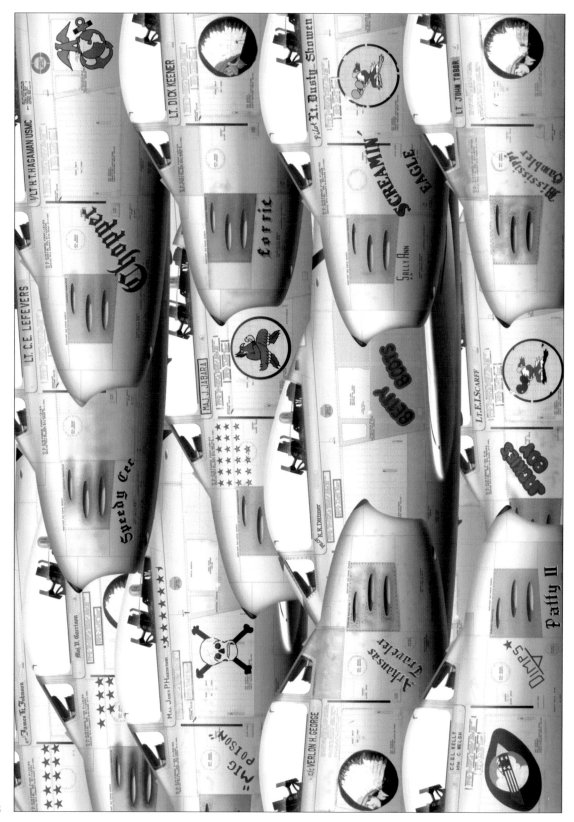

COCKPIT TIME WITH THE ACES

Although 4th FW F-86s began flying combat air patrols in December 1950, a further five months passed before Capt James Jabara claimed his fifth and sixth kills to become the first Sabre ace on 20 May 1951. At that time, the ground war was becoming more stagnant as both sides settled around the 38th Parallel, leaving the US media in-theatre searching for another event that would keep the public back home interested in the Korean War. Capt Jabara, and the subsequent 'ace race', duly filled that void until the conflict finally ended in July 1953.

Four months would pass before the press could covet the 4th FW's next aces. On 9 September 1951, two pilots achieved their fifth kills within 23 minutes of each other. The first was 1Lt Richard Becker of the 334th FS, who, unlike his squadronmate Jabara, had no World War 2 fighter experience to draw on in combat – Jabara had claimed 1.5 kills flying P-51s with the 382nd FS/363rd FG in the ETO in 1944.

Less than 30 minutes later, 335th FS pilot Capt Ralph 'Hoot' Gibson claimed a MiG-15 to register his fifth victory in Korea. Like Becker, Gibson was also a combat neophyte when he reached Korea in November 1950. Here, he recalls some of his experiences over 'MiG Alley' prior to claiming his first victory on 28 June 1951;

'This story starts on 10 April 1951, when I was flying on Capt Nick Farrell's wing along the Yalu. We were heading east about 15 miles south of the river at 25,000 ft. Glancing over at the runway at Antung, I saw two MiG-15s take-off and head to the west. Nick told me to keep an eye on them as we made a 180-degree turn, watching them fly out over the China Sea and then make a turn back to the east.

'By now they were passing through 14,000 ft, and I relayed this information to Nick, but he still couldn't pick them out due to all the ground haze. I called them out two more times as they turned back north, crossing into Manchuria. By this time we were at "bingo" fuel, and we turned south and proceeded back to Suwon AB.

'The reason I mention this uneventful story is that it was my very first sighting of an enemy aircraft. I was unaware at that time that

1Lt Richard Becker holds up four fingers right after returning from the missions that saw him claim his third and fourth kills on 18 August 1951. He would become the second jet ace exactly three weeks later. Becker scored his last three victories (as well as one probable and one damaged) whilst flying F-86A-5 49-1257. This aircraft survived the war and later flew with the 121st FS, which was assigned to the Washington D.C. ANG (*Richard Becker*)

Having just returned from yet another 'MiG Alley' patrol, 1Lt 'Hoot' Gibson takes a few minutes to describe any problems he may have experienced with his jet to his crew chief, Sgt Ormond W Scruggs. Gibson's new-found ace status is marked for all to see on the side of his F-86A-5 (49-1109) (*Don Showen*)

many of these MiGs were being flown by Russian pilots that had seen action in World War 2, whereas only a quarter of our pilots in-theatre had combat time from that conflict.

'I knew then that I would soon be flying as an element lead, which would give me a chance to attack and shoot the MiGs down. For several years prior to reaching the 4th, this was all I had been training for.'

Capt Gibson's first opportunity to engage the enemy came just over a month later, on 20 May, when he was flying element lead in Maj Ben Emmert's flight. Some 15 minutes into the mission, Gibson's wingman, 1Lt Lon Walter, had to abort the flight because of gauge malfunctions. His formation was far enough from MiG territory to allow 1Lt Walter to return home without having to take Gibson with him. This allowed the latter to tag along as a spare, which meant that when the MiGs were sighted and external tanks were jettisoned, if one of the Sabres had a hung tank he would move into that slot. However, when the time came to release the tanks, none hung up. Gibson recalled;

'I asked the other element leader (Capt Milton E Nelson, who would finish his tour with three MiG kills) if I could be a third aircraft in his element, and he duly gave his permission. Seconds later, I called out "MiGs at 'ten o'clock', about 3500 ft ahead of us". As they manoeuvred for our lead element, they started to climb and we followed, closing the gap to about 2500 ft. At the top of the climb, they started to turn back for our lead, and I told Nelson I would take the MiG on the right.

'I shot a burst and got good hits. I think that was the first time that the pilot realised he had an F-86 behind him, because he wobbled his wings looking back at me. He immediately separated from his leader and turned to the right, dropping his nose and taking evasive action. I continued to press the attack, and had several more good hits. He went out of sight in a steep dive, smoking badly, as I turned for home with Capt Nelson.'

After the 4th FW's photo interpreter examined Gibson's gun camera film, it was determined that he had scored close to 1000 hits on the hapless MiG. This was exceptional marksmanship considering that each of the six guns carried approximately 275 rounds. However, since Gibson was fighting without a wingman, he had no one to verify his kill, so he was credited with a 'probable'. Capt Nelson *was* credited with a MiG-15 kill during the mission, however. Of significant note, Capt James Jabara, who also became embroiled with the MiGs during this engagement, scored two kills to make him the 4th FW's first jet ace.

Double kills on missions were fairly common amongst the sharpshooters of the 4th, especially if the MiGs were up in large numbers. Indeed, 'Hoot' Gibson claimed two kills just before midday on 18 June 1951 for his first confirmed victories when a mixed formation of 334th and 336th FS F-86s intercepted a regiment of MiG-15s that chose to fight. Five communist jets were shot down for the loss of a single F-86. Gibson related how the mission unfolded;

'I was element lead for World War 2 ace Lt Col Ben Emmert, who was also our squadron commander, and 1Lt Jim Heckman was flying on my wing. We climbed out at 44,000 ft and made a couple of turns before I spotted some MiGs about 25 miles away. They were at our "three o'clock" as we dropped our external tanks and turned towards them.

'As they got closer, we could see that they were a very large group, and the closure rate between us and them had to be about 1200 mph. We met over 50 of them head-on! One of the MiGs was right out ahead of me, and I turned to attack. As he started down in a hard left turn, I opened fire. Some of my rounds were hitting the MiG's mid-section, but I couldn't pull hard enough to keep my gunsight pipper on him. I asked Heckman if he could take him since he was on my right and would pull fewer Gs to stay on the target. He pressed the attack and I crossed to the right, manoeuvring for position. We were in a hard diving left turn when Jim scored hits on the jet's wing root, fuselage and tail section. The MiG went down and was observed to have crashed into the ground.

'As we turned away from this fight, I spotted another MiG a little low and to the right. I manoeuvred behind it and closed to about 700 ft, since my gunsight had failed in the previous engagement and I could not get it to re-set. I fired a couple of dead centre bursts into the jet and it rolled into an inverted position, with large pieces tearing off the aircraft and smaller bits flying off into its jet wash. One more burst tore the entire right wing off, and it spiralled down and crashed.'

The fight was far from over, however, and Gibson and Heckman started focusing on the action around them. Seconds later, Gibson saw that his squadron commander was being closely pursued by another MiG, so he immediately went to his aid;

'I got within range, and after several evasive manoeuvres I gave him a burst that impacted all over the cockpit, fuselage and wings of his MiG. It quickly burst into flames and went in to an uncontrolled dive and exploded at 3000 ft. Two of the Sabres in our flight were at "bingo" fuel, so they departed for the base while I joined up on the CO's wing to continue the patrol. We locked on to one more MiG and Lt Col

Capt James Jabara poses for a USAF photographer in the cockpit of his jet in the spring of 1951. He saw most of his action during his first tour whilst flying top cover for F-80 and F-84 fighter-bombers (*Bill Graski*)

The names on this sign, hung outside the 335th CO's tent at Suwon AB, list some of the most experienced and capable fighter pilots in-theatre in the summer of 1951. By the time they had completed their combat tours, between them, they had 11.5 confirmed kills. Only 'Bones' Marshall would attain Sabre ace status, however (*A J Walter*)

Emmert quickly shot it down, so it had been a very successful day.

'On the flight back to base, we had to report our kills to Fifth Air Force Control. The CO called in one kill and I had three. During the debriefing, I gave 1Lt Heckman credit for one of my victories because he had poured a lot of rounds into that MiG.

'As a side note to this patrol, this had been Lt Col Emmert's 61st mission in Korea. In World War 2 he had been shot down on his 61st mission.'

Group CO Col Ben Preston (standing, left) and Wing CO Col Harrison Thyng (standing, right) hold up the 4th's latest scoreboard on 15 December 1951. The wing had claimed 13 kills in the previous 48 hours, one of which had fallen to future Sabre ace Thyng. Preston had also got a kill, claiming his fourth, and last, MiG. Standing to Preston's left is 334th FS CO, and ace, Maj George Davis, who claimed two MiGs on 13 December (USAF)

Maj George Davis, Col Ben Preston and Maj Winton Marshall pose for the camera after the 12-kill mission of 30 November 1950. Davis and Marshall had just 'made ace' (USAF)

During the second Korean winter of the war (November 1951 through to April 1952), a full strength Sabre force of two fighter wings dashed any hopes the communists might have had of dominating the airspace between the Yalu River and Pyongyang. With the re-equipment of the 51st FW with F-86Es in December, the doubling of Sabre ranks to 150+ jets in-theatre saw the number of communist aircraft being shot down steadily increase month on month.

Following the 25 successes in October, 26 kills were credited to Sabre pilots in November, 28 (including five to the 51st FW) in December, 32 (27 to the 51st) in January, 17 (ten to the 51st) in February, 39 (14 to the 51st) in March and 44 (25 to the 51st) in April.

Three more 4th FW pilots also achieved Sabre ace status during this period, with Maj Richard Creighton (336th FS) claiming his fifth victory on 27 November 1951, and Majs George Davis (334th FS) and Winton Marshall (335th FS) following suit three days later.

An increasing number of MiGs in-theatre and the stalemate in the peace talks at Panmunjom were the primary reasons why Sabre pilots enjoyed rich pickings during the second winter of the war. The stalemate caused the FEAF's Fifth Air Force to turn up the pressure on the communist negotiators by increasing the number of bombing sorties against targets along the Yalu River, regardless of the nearby MiG threat. This translated into more sorties for the F-86 squadrons and many more dogfights between the two fighter types as they struggled to achieve air superiority.

DEATH OF AN ACE

Undoubtedly the standout Sabre pilot in Korea during this high-

Maj Richard D Creighton (left) and his armourer, Sgt George O'Brien, smile for the camera prior to the former flying a mission on 5 January 1952. The temperature at Kimpo at the time was hovering around freezing, as it did for much of the winter months in Korea. Creighton had already claimed all seven of his MiG kills by the time this shot was taken (*George O'Brien*)

His helmet marked with the 334th FS badge, 1Lt William Littlefield was flying as Maj George Davis's wingman on the day the ace was killed in combat (*William Littlefield*)

scoring period over the winter of 1951-52 was the CO of the 334th FS, Maj George Davis. A seven-kill P-47 ace from World War 2 (he had flown Thunderbolts in the Pacific with the 342nd FS/348th FG in 1943-45), Davis had joined the 4th FW in October 1951. Claiming his first victories on 27 November, he 'made ace' for a second time on 30 November when he downed three Tu-2s and a MiG-15. Fond of scoring multiple kills, Davis claimed two more MiG victories on 5 December and no less than four eight days later.

The first double ace in Korea, Davis set off on his 59th mission on the morning of 10 February 1952. Leading yet another combat air patrol over 'MiG Alley', he quickly destroyed two enemy aircraft to take his tally to 14, but was then himself shot down and killed by a third communist fighter. Had he lived, Davis might well have been the war's top scoring ace. 1Lt William W Littlefield was his wingman on this ill-fated mission;

'Maj Davis and I broke away from the rest of the patrol just north of Sinanju. We headed straight for the Yalu to attack MiGs reported to be heading south across the river. About ten miles from the mouth of the Yalu, but still over North Korea, we spotted a gaggle of about ten MiG-15s coming into the "alley". They were about 800 ft below us, and Maj Davis called for a diving turn that would bring us behind them. As we closed in, he started firing at the MiG at the rear of the formation. I saw the enemy's wing root light up from the Major's 0.50-cal hits. Billowing smoke immediately poured out of the stricken fighter, and it went into an uncontrolled dive towards the ground.

'Maj Davis called out to make sure I was still with him, and we continued right through the formation. He quickly lined up another MiG near the front. His fire impacted all over its right wing root, and like the first one, it started smoking and went straight down in a dive. By this time we had worked our way through the entire formation and were out in front of the remaining MiGs. We were in a very hazardous position, but Maj Davis slowed down to take on the closest MiG. Evidently, one of their pilots had a clean shot at him, and the Major's jet took at least one or two 37 mm cannon hits. It went out of control and crashed into a mountain about 30 miles south of the Yalu River.'

Records show that Maj Davis was flying F-86E-10 51-2752 at the time. He was later awarded a posthumous Medal of Honor for his exploits on this final mission. In an unusual move, the Chinese broadcast details of the pilot reported to have shot him down. He was named as 'the famous air hero Chiang Chi Huei'. This came several weeks after Davis's last mission, but was the first indication of his fate. It also opened up fresh speculation about the identity of the MiG pilots, and strongly suggested that some of the air regiments were Chinese-manned. But nationality was not an issue. What concerned the American pilots was that there were more MiGs in the sky now than ever before, and that they were being aggressively flown.

Another talented pilot to fall victim to communist fighters in 1952 was 336th FS CO Maj Felix Asla, who had four confirmed kills to his credit at the time of his death (in F-86E 51-2767) on 1 August. 1Lt W P Dunbar was one of the young 336th FS pilots that had flown several missions on Maj Asla's wing during the spring and summer of 1952, and he was over 'MiG Alley' at the time his CO was shot down by a MiG-15;

'I was up on the same mission that day, but in another flight. Naturally, when the action heated up, you tended to focus on your element leader and yourself, so we were not fully aware of what another flight was doing. The MiGs were out that day, and my lead went after one of them, with me in trail. I followed him in a Mach 1 dive from 35,000 ft down to about 15,000 ft as he attempted to get onto the tail of an enemy jet. I must have endured about 7 Gs in the pull-up and turn in order to stay with my leader. At that point, the MiG's nose pointed straight up, and it climbed away in a 180-degree turn to well over 40,000 ft. My section lead never got within 3000 ft of him.

'After we returned to Kimpo, my flight leader asked me if I had seen a MiG shoot down an F-86, and I said I had not. This was understandable because I was flying in an F-86A, and at those speeds and Gs, you didn't have a chance to observe anything except trying to keep your lead's tail clear. At our debriefing, it became clear as to what had happened to Maj Asla. A MiG-15 had managed to get in behind him and shoot the left wing off of his jet, and in all the action, none of us had reported seeing a 'chute.

'His death remained a mystery until we started piecing together the radio chatter and figured out that he thought the MiG was his wingman, who had become separated from him. Asla was making a slow turn to the left at the time, and the MiG was in a perfect join-up position. He was also in a perfect position to shoot. It would not have taken much of a sharpshooter to have shot Asla down. It was a tragic loss for the squadron.'

This F-86E-10 was the mount of 336th FS CO Maj Felix Asla, who was credited with four kills in 1952. Nicknamed *THE CHOPPER*, 51-2767 is seen here displaying a total of eight kills – Asla also had damaged claims marked up on the jet. He was killed when shot down in this very aircraft on 1 August 1952, just days after this photograph was taken in late July (*William Thomas*)

Maj Felix Asla (centre, standing to attention) has just been awarded the DFC and Silver Star by 4th FW CO, Col Harrison Thyng, for outstanding leadership of the 336th FS in mid 1952 (*Gordon Beem*)

Three months prior to his demise, Maj Asla had witnessed at first hand the destructive power of the MiG-15's trio of cannons when his wingman, 1Lt John E Dews, fell victim to a communist fighter whilst participating in his third sortie on 1 April 1952. Most 4th FW pilots flew missions on a rotational basis, which meant a few hours off after each mission. However, there were times when the workload prevented this luxury, and many of them flew two, and occasionally three, missions in a day. 1Lt Dews was one of those pilots;

'It was one of the busiest days I would ever have in combat, and my Form-5 shows I flew three missions that day. Maj Asla was my flight leader and I was in the No 2 slot, with my call-sign being "John Red Two". Somewhere northeast of Sinuiju, Asla and I spotted MiGs that were just south of the river. He immediately engaged the flight of four enemy jets from astern, while I did what wingmen do – keeping lead's "six o'clock" clear.

'Out of nowhere, three MiGs came up behind Asla, and I called for a "hard break to the left", which we both executed. I had gone about 60 degrees into my break when my Sabre was hit by three cannon rounds. From what I could instantly assess, two of them had hit my left wing and the third had struck my tail assembly. I never saw my adversary, but Maj Asla later told me that the "shooter" was the leader of a flight of four MiGs that had dropped down on us just as we entered the left turn. They had to attack me because Asla was too far up ahead, and there was no way he could get back to prevent the pass on me.'

Pilots from the 4th FW dine in at Kimpo AB with the commanding general in the autumn of 1952. Sitting against the wall in the centre is group CO, and ace, Col Royal N Baker. To his left is 4th FW CO, and fellow ace, Col James K Johnson, whilst to his right is Fifth Air Force CO, Lt Gen Glenn O Barcus. The latter flew several combat missions with the 4th FW in 1952-53 (*USAF*)

Both 'making ace' within 30 minutes of each other in the late afternoon of 3 May 1952, 16th FS/51st FW pilot Maj Donald Adams (left) shakes hands with Capt Robert Latshaw of the 335th FS. Adams had claimed his two MiGs near Yongampo at 1730 hrs and Latshaw had destroyed his, in the F-86E-1 parked behind them, at 1800 hrs near Yangsi. Both aces would subsequently perish in flying accidents after returning home (*USAF*)

336th FS armourer Sgt George O'Brien busily loads belts of 0.50-cal API into the magazine of Maj Richard Creighton's Sabre. The turnaround times between missions for F-86s at Kimpo was relatively quick due to the vast experience of the groundcrews stationed at the base (*George O'Brien*)

1Lt Dews was flying one of the older F-86Es (50-586) in the squadron, and he was at 34,000 ft when he was hit. His Sabre immediately fell into a violent spin, which lasted until he was at about 9500 ft;

'When I radioed "Red Leader One" that I had been hit, he broke off and quickly engaged the MiG that had fired on me. He did not get a visual on me as I was spinning down, but he did acknowledge my transmissions. My F-86 finally gained some form of flight when I slowed it down by reducing power, popping my dive brakes and entering the denser air at a lower altitude. At Maj Asla's suggestion, I set a course for Chodo Island, where, with good luck, I bailed out and was quickly recovered by helicopter. My F-86 fell into the sea shortly after I exited the cockpit.'

MORE GROUND-POUNDING

During the spring of 1952, the FEAF realised just how efficient the Chinese were in quickly rebuilding destroyed or damaged targets. It also observed the rapid movement of highly mobile heavier calibre anti-aircraft guns throughout North Korea. The latter could be positioned alongside key railway lines, roads and bridges, depending on where they were needed most. F-84s and aging F-80s and F-51s were charged with inflicting major damage on such targets, and the vulnerable fighter-bombers in turn relied on the Sabres to afford them protection from the now ever-present MiGs.

The F-86 wings were always the 'go to' units when there was any threat against the fighter-bombers working from Pyongyang north to the river. As the number of F-84s in particular increased in-theatre from the early spring of 1952 onwards, the pressure once again shifted back onto the communists, as just about any viable target that cropped up in North Korea was quickly attacked. Attempts to intercept the fighter-bombers soon became sporadic at best, with the MiG pilots finding that they could not take the F-84s and F-80s on due to the very effective barrier patrols set up by the F-86s flying at altitude ahead of them.

The communist pilots duly reverted to employing their three favourite tactics (the 'Yo-Yo', 'End Run' and 'Decoy') that occasionally gave them success. Indeed, these manoeuvres allowed the MiGs to elude the F-86s on at least four occasions when the fighter-bombers were up in force during the spring and summer of 1952, the enemy penetrating south of 'MiG Alley'. Yet despite getting in amongst the fighter-bombers, the MiG pilots did not score anywhere near the number of kills they should have primarily due to over eagerness, poor gunnery and inept manoeuvring at close quarters.

No fewer than seven pilots from the 4th FW secured their fifth kills during this period, with six of them hailing from the high-scoring 335th FS. The first of these was veteran aviator, and Air National Guardsman, Capt Robert J Love, who became the 11th jet ace of the war with two MiG victories on 21 April. Flying on Love's wing on three of his MiG-15-killing missions was 1Lt Martin J Bambrick, who reflected on his combat experiences with Capt Love;

'He and I were assigned to "C Flight" at about the same time, Love having wangled a transfer to the wing from his California Air National Guard unit (the F-84-equipped 196th FBS, which had been mobilised in July 1951 and assigned to the 116th FBW, based at Misawa AB, Japan) at the end of his tour. He was an excellent shooter, and any mission I flew with him proved to be very interesting.

'There was one (on 20 March 1952) where Love locked onto the tail of a MiG, and its pilot could not shake him. In the seconds that followed, he fired all of his ammunition, and there is no telling how many rounds hit that MiG. It continued to fly straight and level, and there was no fire or smoke from the multiple hits. We both moved up and bracketed the MiG on either side, almost flying close formation with it. The pilot was apparently dead, or at least pretending to be. I asked Bob if he wanted me to get into a position to finish him off, and he replied in the negative as the pilot was already dead. We left the MiG to return to the action. Later on, it was confirmed to us that that communist jet had indeed lost altitude in a glide and crashed into the ground some distance off to the west. This helped confirm the kill for Love.

'Four days later (on 24 March), I was on his wing again. This time, I was concentrating so much on keeping his "six o'clock" clear that I was not paying any attention to where he was shooting. I can't remember if we had another element with us at the time. It was probably just the two of us, or they had split off when chasing a MiG. I was aware that Love was bearing down on another jet, so I was keeping an eye on several others that

335th FS pilot 1Lt Martin Bambrick peers through a large hole in the wing of his Sabre made by a 37 mm cannon round fired from a MiG-15 in June 1952 (*Martin Bambrick*)

335th FS pilot Capt Robert Love became the USAF's 11th jet ace on 3 May 1952 (*USAF*)

Part of the 335th FS's notorious 'D Flight', 1Lt James Kasler was its first member to 'make ace'. He claimed his fourth and fifth MiG-15 kills on 15 May 1952, thus becoming the USAF's 15th jet ace (*USAF*)

'Aces High'! All three units, as well as the group HQ, are represented by the pilots in this photograph. No fewer than 37 communist aircraft were destroyed by these four individuals between 8 May 1952 and 13 March 1953. They are, from left to right, 2Lt James Low (335th FS, 9 kills), Capt Robinson Risner (336th FS, 8 kills), Col Royal Baker (4th FG HQ, 13 kills) and Capt Leonard Lilley (334th FS, 7 kills) (*USAF*)

were close by. They were capable of making a pass on us within seconds, so I could not divert any of my attention to what Love was up to.

'After closing well within range, he fired several short bursts into the doomed aircraft, and as I finally glanced over in that direction, the MiG pilot ejected. By this time, much of my attention was on Love, and his kill. Within seconds of the ejection, he made a couple of circles around the parachuting pilot and then lined up for a pass. My first thought was that Love was going to fire on the enemy pilot, but he only turned his camera on to verify the fact that his MiG was now without a pilot, which would count as a kill. I am sure that the pilot was scared to death as Love's F-86 bore down on him.'

Discussing the third kill mission that he flew with Capt Love, 1Lt Bambrick reiterates just how good a marksman the ace was;

'We were up on a late afternoon combat air patrol, and there wasn't much enemy activity. About mid-way through our mission, we encountered a lone MiG south of the Yalu, and he was heading north toward Antung. We had the altitude advantage, so our closure rate was very good. Either the pilot did not see us or he froze up, because Capt Love came right in at an angle from the rear and I was covering his backside close in, so I had a good view. Love called out "Watch this. I'm going to hit him right in his airspeed indicator – now!" He fired a short burst, and sure enough the rounds converged all over the front of the cockpit area.

'Several seconds later, he stated that he was going to fire the next burst and take out the MiG's altimeter. The tracers duly converged in front of the cockpit once again. It was superb shooting from about 700 ft out. The MiG did not waver, its nose instead slowly dropping at an ever increasing angle until the jet hit the ground. The pilot never bailed out, so the first burst probably got him. It was some of the best marksmanship I ever saw in the F-86.'

DEADLY 'D FLIGHT'

Capt Love's contemporaries within the 335th FS's 'D Flight' at this time were just as aggressive. Indeed, collectively, they had an 'attitude', which led them to devise their own emblem embodying a caricature of their unit CO, Maj Philip Van Sickle. The group included Capt Philip E Colman (four kills) and 1Lts Coy L Austin (two), James H Kasler (15th jet ace, on 15 May 1952, with six kills) and James F Low (17th jet ace, on 15 June 1952, with nine kills). 1Lt Albert Smiley (three kills) also flew with this elite group;

'I got my first MiG-15 (on 8 May 1952) when I was flying on Coy Austin's wing. I spotted him and Austin didn't, so he told me to take it – that was our standard policy at the time. It seemed that I chased that MiG all over North Korea. Every time I had him lined up, he

would pull up into an abrupt, fast vertical climb, stall out and then flip over on his back. I took several shots at him, and I'm not sure how many rounds hit him squarely. I think the pilot probably ejected out of frustration! Anyway, Austin verified that the pilot was in his 'chute, so I got the kill.

'With my second (on 15 May 1952), I was still flying wing. Phil Colman was leading the flight and Kasler was leading the element. It was a repeat scenario of my first kill. Kasler first spotted the MiGs over Antung. "Casey" Colman still hadn't spotted them, so he told Kasler to take them. I was flying Kasler's wing. In a matter of minutes he'd lined up on one of the MiGs, which was apparently getting ready for the landing pattern at Antung.

'As I saw Kasler scoring hits on his target, this MiG came out of nowhere and slid in behind him. He was lining up to fire when I radioed Kasler to break. Either he didn't hear me or he ignored me, as he kept on firing at his MiG. The only thing I could do was to fire a quick warning burst in the general direction of the second MiG to get his attention. I wasn't looking through my sights when I pulled the trigger, but my rounds impacted all over the enemy fighter. He was lighting up pretty good from all of the API rounds that were hitting him.

'The next thing I knew, the MiG's canopy popped off, the seat came out and there was the pilot floating back toward me, sitting in his seat. He passed by my left wing. My rate of closure wasn't too fast, so I banked over

F-86E-1 50-623 *Pretty Mary and The J's* was the personal mount of 4th FW CO Col Harrison Thyng. On 20 May 1952 he scored his fifth kill to become the USAF's 16th jet ace (*Harry Thyng*)

Other than the seven *Gunval* Sabres trialled by the 4th FW in early 1953, every F-86 committed to the war was armed with six rapid-firing 0.50-cal Browning machine guns. Although they did not have the instant knock-down power of the MiG-15's three cannon, they could accurately strike a small area over and over again. Ordnance crews continually serviced the guns to keep them operable (*Jimmie Pierce*)

to get a good look at him. Apparently, his helmet had come off in the ejection. He had long blond hair, with what we used to call a "white side-walled" haircut, which meant that the hair was clipped down to bare skin about an inch or so above the ears. He had to be East German or Russian. I never saw a 'chute, and my altitude when I passed by him was less than 500 ft. Kasler got two confirmed kills on this mission, which made him the 15th jet ace of the war.'

The last of the seven 4th FW aces crowned during this period was the 335th FS's Capt Clifford Jolley, who claimed three kills in two days on 7 and 8 August. Like Capt Robert Love, Jolley was also an ex-Guardsman from the 196th FBW. His F-86, appropriately named *Jolley Roger*, was well known within the ranks of the wing.

Having flown many piston-engined types in the mid to late 1940s, Jolley was accepted into jet school at Williams AFB in 1948 as an Air National Guard pilot, and he subsequently served with units in California and Utah. Sent to the jet combat gunnery school at Nellis AFB soon after being recalled to active duty in March 1951, Jolley was assigned to the 4th FW, and the rest is history. Here, he recalls some of his early experiences in the Sabre, and also his clashes with MiG-15s over 'MiG Alley';

'Up to 0.95 Mach, the F-86A handled like a Piper Cub at 80 mph. However, at 0.95001 Mach, the jet developed a very noticeable wing roll tendency that would continue until you reached mach one. After that speed was achieved, the aircraft flew smoothly and responded to the controls, except that it felt like the stick was in cement!

'The newer F-86Es started arriving in the Far East at around the same time that I did, and my first experience with one was in Korea. The jet's controls were all hydraulic, with no boost cables as in the A-model, and instead of the control stick operating the elevators, it operated the entire horizontal stabiliser, with the elevators linked so as to accentuate the action! The trim actions in both cases served to "centre" the stick to maintain your desired position, so hydraulic pressure was only applied to whichever side you directed the stick.

'In a combat situation, we always had the element leaders flying in the A-models whenever possible so as to be sure that those pilots following could keep up! I can vividly recall being in an awkward position in an F-86A, trying desperately to shoot a MiG off the tail of a pilot flying evasive manoeuvres in an E-model. I can tell you that it was a monumental physical accomplishment just staying with these two aircraft, let alone shooting the MiG down. Fortunately, I was in excellent physical shape.'

At this stage in the war the MiGs still reigned supreme when it came to having an altitude advantage. The communists fully exploited this too by sending large formations of 'students' over 'MiG Alley' so that they could observe what the F-86s were doing without putting themselves at risk. This safe haven was compromised, however, when the new F-86Fs began to reach Korea in September 1952, although even this latest version of the Sabre was still at the top end of its performance envelope when it came to intercepting high-flying MiGs above 48,000 ft.

In an effort to solve these problems, the FEAF ordered the 4th FW to fit five of its new F-86Fs with a belly pod that housed three jet-assisted take-off bottles (JATO). Capt Jolley was one of the few pilots permitted to fly these Sabres;

'We received five of these modified F-models, whose pod-mounted JATO bottles (permanently fitted to the aircraft) could be fired in a series or all at the same time. This device gave us a seven-second burst, which meant rapid closure on MiGs that were up at an altitude we were having difficulty attaining. Only the four most experienced pilots in the squadron were selected to fly missions where JATO was likely to be used. These special F-models were tail heavy, and they started "porpoising" at about 35,000 ft if you let the speed drop below 0.78 Mach.

'Although my last two MiG-15 kills were made using the pod, I am sure that I would have been just as successful without JATO assistance, as the tail-heavy mush-out I experienced when I performed a "Split-S" manoeuvre to initiate the attacks almost saw me lose contact with the MiGs.'

Although not entirely won over by the JATO modification, Jolley was certainly sold on the Sabre as a gunnery platform. Its gunsight was radar-activated, and this gave the pilot accurate information about his distance from the target. It would also automatically calculate the lead required to make the kill. A target could be released from the gunsight once locked up through a simple push of a button, and another target then selected. By holding the reticule on the target and watching the range drum, most pilots would open fire at 3000 ft and typically score effective hits on their prey.

The six 0.50-cal machine guns in the Sabre's nose would fire at a rate of about 3000 rounds per minute, and one short burst, which would equate to about ten rounds per gun, was sufficient to make a respectable hole in a MiG. The F-86's wing magazines were typically loaded with two lead ball rounds, two API and one tracer in groups of five. The weapons were also fitted with air chargers to retract and reload rounds should a 'short' shell cause a misfire, which seldom happened.

1Lt Martin Bambrick, wingman for many of the 4th FW's aces, recalled Capt Jolley's expertise in the cockpit of a Sabre;

'I flew with Capt Jolley many times, but since I was an element lead in the second section, I did not get the opportunity to take too close a look at what he did. I do remember one mission, however, where I was flying in the No 4 slot and Jolley was No 1. I was on the left of the flight, scanning everything in that direction to make sure that we were not surprised. I happened to glance forward, and I saw a MiG coming straight for my formation some 50 ft below us. Before I could say anything, he had raced by, the MiG being painted metallic green overall. I called a break to the left and down, trying to get a glimpse of it, but never did. Due to the colour of the MiG and the terrain below, it was very difficult to see, and Jolley stated that he had not spotted it.

'The MiG pilot may not have seen us either, as he left the area as soon as he could. We did some "figure-eights" around the area, but there wasn't another aircraft to be seen. This had been an unusual encounter.

'A few days later we were up again, flying extremely high, and this time we all had binoculars. We were literally floating along at 45,000+ ft. All of a sudden, about 150 ft in front of us, were two huge flak bursts! They were ominous looking, with bright orange fire in their centre. At that altitude flak was unheard of, and we immediately altered our course a little to the

left and the radar directed anti-aircraft artillery never corrected for our change. This was the only time that I encountered flak at such a high altitude.

'One of the most memorable missions that I was involved in with Capt Jolley saw me in the No 3 slot in a flight of four that he was leading. Jolley was always very aggressive in his dealings with MiGs, and it paid off for him. We were patrolling high over "MiG Alley" when one of the guys in our flight called out a single MiG well below us. The enemy pilot had evidently seen us and was making a high speed run to get north of the Yalu. Jolley pitched over and went after him.

'He didn't drop his speed brakes at the time, but he did jettison his external tanks! He initiated a very tight spiral, like a continuous barrel roll, almost straight down to get behind this guy, who was probably 10,000-12,000 ft below us. When all of this started, we were probably at about 35,000 ft. Jolley's wingman finally called out that he couldn't stay with him in such a tight manoeuvre. I managed to hook up with him, however, keeping my hand on my G-suit valve button to keep it inflated all the way down so that I would not black out from all the Gs.'

The MiG pilot was determined to make it back to his base, and he slid right into the landing pattern. Capt Jolley was equally as determined not to let up. To avoid the flak batteries ringing the base, he and Bambrick descended to treetop level, where there was less chance of being hit. Quickly losing sight of their target because they had dropped so low, the only way to lock the MiG back up was to gain some altitude. Having climbed again, they found themselves positioned right over the end of the runway, with numerous small-calibre AAA winking at them.

The MiG Jolley wanted was not in sight, and their priorities quickly

F-86E-10 51-2834 was used to great effect by Capt Clifford Jolley in the summer of 1952, as the eight victory markings just aft of the guns clearly reveal. By the time this photograph was taken in the spring of 1953, Jolley had returned home and his jet had been transferred to the 336th FS (*Houston Tuel*)

Right
Capt Clifford Jolley became the USAF's 18th jet ace on 8 August 1952. Both his helmet and his jet were marked with pirate flags (*Karl Dittmer*)

Armed and fuelled, two flights of Sabres from the 334th FS wait for their pilots to strap in and fire up their turbojet engines at Kimpo AB in the autumn of 1952 (*Bill Littlefield*)

shifted as they flew down the runway, pulling streamers off of their canopies. Their only means of escape was to stay low and head out over the Yellow Sea at a height of just 25 ft. Both pilots survived without a scratch, and the incident probably spawned numerous stories among the communist gunners on the ground.

Jolley's eventful clashes with MiGs in August 1952 were typical of the dozens of engagements that took place on a near-daily basis during the first nine days of the month. On the 4th, ex-wingman 1Lt Henry Crescibene of the 335th FS claimed the sole MiG-15 to be destroyed;

'We were lead on a 16-ship patrol that day by group CO, Col Royal N Baker. A future double MiG ace, he was vastly experienced in aerial combat thanks to his experiences, and kills, in World War 2. I was flying element leader for Capt Karl Dittmer, who was my flight leader (Dittmer had claimed a MiG kill three days earlier).

'After an hour of cruising at 30,000 ft at high Mach, I thought I spotted a couple of MiG-15s in the distance, and asked permission to go down and take a look. My wingman and I dived down to where I thought my MiGs were, only to find the sky empty. At that point I throttled back because my fuel gauges were showing that it was time to return home. Moments later Col Baker radioed for our gaggle to head south back to Kimpo.

'I decided to hang around a bit longer, and within a few minutes I saw three MiGs in front and some 10,000 ft below us. I got on the radio and asked if there were any F-86s in this area other than my wingman, and Col Baker replied

New Sabres usually arrived at Kisarazu AB, in Japan, before they were flown to units in South Korea. Both destined for the 4th FW, these two F-86E-10s survived the war and were later assigned to other units after their combat tours (*Cale Herry*)

63

that the rest of the Sabres were out of the area and en route to base.

'With my fuel getting dangerously low, I told my wingman to remain at altitude while I dove down and made one firing pass on the MiGs. I would then break right and join up with him, prior to heading back south. During my dive, I had to roll upside down and perform a "Split-S" so as to keep the enemy formation in sight. As I was approaching the jets that I was focused on, another seven MiGs popped up out of nowhere, but I continued to press home my attack. By this time I was doing about 575 knots at 20,000 ft. Coming in on them slightly below their altitude, I was able to get a good burst into the MiGs' underside where their fuel tanks were.

'I started firing at a range of 600-800 ft, scoring numerous hits on the underside of one of the MiGs. At the same time I spotted orange tracer rounds flying past me – I was being fired on by one of the other MiGs. The gap narrowed as I continued to fire, and suddenly my target exploded in a ball of fire. I immediately broke hard right and almost collided with another MiG. Fortunately, none of them followed me, and I was able to join up with my wingman and head for Kimpo.

'I wasn't sure that I would have enough fuel for a safe landing, so once we got up to altitude I retarded the throttle to use minimal fuel. By restricting my consumption, I managed to make it back to base safely, although I barely made it to the ramp before my engine flamed out. When we examined my F-86, we found a piece of the MiG-15 that I had shot down lodged in the right side of the aircraft's nose – this had struck my jet when I almost flew through the explosion. The debris left no doubt that I had indeed destroyed a MiG, and I was duly credited with a kill!'

One of the biggest clashes during this period was fought on 6 August, when 52 MiG-15s engaged 35 Sabres in a one-sided dogfight that saw six communist fighters destroyed. By the end of August, there had been sightings of 1155 MiGs during this month alone, with enough close-in contact between the two fighters to net 34 enemy jets shot down for the loss of two F-86s in aerial combat. Things remained just as hot over 'MiG Alley' the following month.

In fact September proved to be a banner month for Sabre kills in the Korean War, with no fewer than 64 MiG-15s being claimed destroyed (this tally was only bettered by the 78 claimed in June 1953). Some 1857 airborne sightings were made by Sabre pilots, who were working overtime to protect round-the-clock UN fighter-bomber sorties targeting communist forces attempting to head south to reinforce frontline positions.

The worst day of the month for the Sabres was 4 September, when large numbers of enemy fighters darted back and forth across the Yalu in a series of slashing attacks on patrolling F-86s. Fighting literally a running gun battle in true 'wild west' style, the Sabre pilots ended the day with 13 MiGs kills for the loss of four F-86s (half the number lost that month). Emerging from the carnage of 4 September was the war's 19th Sabre ace, Maj Frederick 'Boots' Blesse of the 334th FS. Over the next four weeks he would add five more victories to his tally before ending his tour.

336th FS pilot Capt Robinson Risner downed two MiG-15s on 21 September to take his score to six victories – he would eventually leave Korea at the end of January 1953 with eight kills to his credit. A probable

The very last ace of the Korean War, 1Lt Charles Cleveland had to wait until April 2000 for his probable claim of 21 September 1952 to be upgraded to confirmed. He thus became the USAF's 40th Sabre ace (*Charles Cleveland*)

Maintained by the 336th FS, F-86E-10 51-2822 was assigned to 4th FG CO Col Royal N Baker, who scored several of his 13 kills with it. The jet survived the conflict and saw post-war duty with the 35th FW in Japan (*Richard Hintermeier*)

Despite the weather in the Korean Peninsula being bitterly cold in the winter and extremely hot in the summer, pilots still had to man the alert jets 24 hours a day. This shot was taken on the alert pad at Kimpo AB in the spring, when the weather was at its mildest. These 335th FS F-86s had to be airborne in minutes should a call come in (*R M Jones*)

victory claimed that same day by 334th FS pilot 1Lt Charles Cleveland would have great significance 47 years later when, on 11 April 2000, the claim was upgraded to confirmed by the American Fighter Aces Association Victory Confirmation Board. Combined with four other confirmed kills credited to Cleveland in August and September 1952, this victory gave him ace status almost five decades after he had achieved the feat!

The wing's next two aces scored their fifth victories within 24 hours of each other on 17 and 18 November 1952. Col Royal Baker (who had claimed 3.5 kills in World War 2) got his fifth victory on the 17th, and would down a further eight MiGs before leaving the wing in mid March 1953. On 18 November Capt Leonard Lilley of the 334th FS claimed a MiG-15 to give him 'ace status'. He would ultimately fly 101 combat missions, finishing his tour in January 1953 with seven victories.

MiG MONITORING

During the second half of 1952, Sabre pilots in Korea were painfully aware of just how much effort the communists were putting into increasing the number of MiGs in-theatre. By year-end, FEAF Intelligence estimates put the overall figure at about 850 jets, which were either in Manchuria already, or available to be rotated in with very little notice.

The four airfields in the Antung Complex (Fen Chen, Takishan, Tatungkou and Antung itself) had been expanded over a two-year period so as to handle the increasing numbers. In addition to this capacity, there were three other major airfields (Anshan, Liaoyang and Mukden) further north into Manchuria, but close enough to service immediate requirements over 'MiG Alley'. Most of these had been built by the Japanese in the early 1940s, and many improvements had been made to them during the current conflict. These seven bases could potentially rival anything that the USSR had in its western defence sectors in Europe.

With high-flying manned reconnaissance aircraft and satellite surveillance systems still some way off, the USAF found it very difficult to keep tabs on what was going on north of Antung. As late as September 1952, the communists were still adding to, or building, new airfields in Manchuria, and most these were far enough north of the Yalu to remain relatively secret.

A lot of the time, F-86 pilots illegally overflying Manchuria in search of MiGs to shoot down made crucial discoveries relating to new bases under construction. Numerous such flights were made by double ace Maj Frederick 'Boots' Blesse during his six-month tour with the 334th FS in 1952;

'At this time the peace talks were going on, and we all knew that the communists were stockpiling MiGs close to the border. We also knew that if an agreement was reached, they could fly a couple of hundred fighters into North Korea at the last minute and have a full-sized air force ready to go. These facts made us keep our eyes open when we were at altitude above the river, or if we strayed north a little.

'One spring afternoon whilst flying over Manchuria, where I should not have been, I noticed some markings on the ground near a little place called Fen Chen that looked like a new runway. After getting back to Kimpo, I grabbed an intelligence officer I knew fairly well, swore him

Maj Frederick 'Boots' Blesse (10 Sabre kills) poses at a post-Korea airshow in Virginia with his childhood hero, Capt Eddie Rickenbacker, who was the leading American ace of World War 1 with 26 victories (*Frederick Blesse*)

to secrecy and told him what I saw. He asked me to keep an eye on it, so once a week I would slip into Manchuria to see what had been accomplished.

'Over the next month or so I watched that place grow from a few scratches in the ground to a 6000-ft cement runway, complete with pre-fab buildings and aircraft being worked on – and they were all MiG-15s! This was going on in three other areas I was monitoring, so by the time the month of May rolled around they had the capacity to launch between 600 and 700 MiGs. At that time we had a total of about 150 to 225 Sabres in the entire theatre to oppose them. Many of our aircraft were out of commission due to a lack of spare parts and for various other reasons.'

On the afternoon of 14 January 1953, 334th FS pilots Capts Manuel Fernandez and Leonard Lilley both claimed MiG kills within three minutes of each other. This was Lilley's seventh, and last, victory during a combat tour that spanned 101 missions, but for Fernandez, it was only his fourth victory. Ironically, the latter pilot was flying Lilley's F-86E-10 51-2764 when he scored his kill, the crew chief outlining the feat in the gun powder residue that collected around the gun ports. Lilley was flying F-86E-1 50-625 on this date, this veteran jet having previously been the mount of 335th FS ace Maj Winton Marshall in late 1951 (*Larry Hendel*)

Very occasionally, the Sabre wings were given permission to overfly the four large MiG bases in the Antung Complex. Such missions were conducted in the early summer and autumn of 1952, as well as the spring of 1953, as part of several massive air efforts by the Fifth Air Force to destroy major communist targets just south of the Yalu River. In order to protect the massed ranks of fighter-bombers sent to attack these targets, and knowing that escorting Sabres would be heavily outnumbered by intercepting communist fighters, the FEAF authorised the employment of unusual tactics so as to ensure the success of these missions, and to reduce the risk of an effective MiG intervention.

Maj 'Boots' Blesse remembered one such mission in which he played a part;

'Just prior to a large attack up in the most dangerous area of North Korea, four of us flight leaders were called in and told about a mission scheduled for the next day that was going to involve three entire fighter-bomber groups (nine squadrons). There was a possibility that they would have to face 400+ MiGs, and we were tasked with keeping these aircraft on the ground until the fighter-bombers had finished and turned back to their bases. The 4th FW was limited in the number of Sabres it could put up, so for this unusual assignment we were given only one flight (four F-86s) apiece to cover each of the four MiG bases in question. I took the airfield at Fen Chen for my flight.'

The rules that Maj Blesse was briefed on for the mission were strict and to the point. The Sabre pilots were not allowed to do any strafing of aircraft on the ground, and they were also not to let any of the MiGs take off. Each flight was to keep the communist jets grounded for 18 minutes, which was how long the fighter-bombers needed to get in, destroy their targets and get out.

Blesse had good knowledge of Fen Chen and the terrain surrounding the base, so he did not require much of a detailed briefing. The Chinese were using radar effectively, and they would know when the F-86s were coming and when the fighter-bombers were nearing their targets.

Two of the 4th's top commanders show the unit's colours during an awards ceremony at Kimpo AB in 1953. Group CO Col Royal N Baker finished his tour with 13 kills, whilst wing CO Col James K Johnson claimed 10 victories (*USAF*)

Accurate time-keeping was going to be critically important to the overall success of the mission. Blesse continued;

'I timed it so that my flight arrived in the area about 20 minutes before the strike began. It would be easy to tell when our fighter-bombers were getting close because the MiGs would start taxiing out for take-off. Sure enough, a few minutes later about 40 to 50 of them started moving all at the same time – nose to tail! We circled the base at 18,000 ft and watched until the first two MiGs started their run-up for take-off. It was easy to tell that the pilots had opened their throttles because of all the debris blowing away behind the jets. This was the cue for me to take my wingman and dive down.

'I could see both MiGs start their take-off roll, and initially it looked like I had mis-timed my pass. Someone in the control tower was on my side, however, and he must have told the communist pilots that they had F-86s on finals. I could see the blue smoke from the MiGs' tyres as the pilots applied brakes in a panic, but they were in that no-man's land without enough room to stop. Their leader and his wingman went right off the end of the runway, then past the field boundary, breaking off both nose gears. What a beautiful sight – two tail pipes sticking up in the air about 100 ft off the end of the Fen Chen runway.'

The effect of seeing a flight of 334th FS Sabres orbiting overhead, and assuming that any jets that took off would be shot down as soon as they retracted their gear, immediately shut down the base's flight plans. Maj Blesse's formation pulled up to 15,000 ft without firing a shot and began their orbit. Strangely enough, all of the MiGs taxied back in and shut down.

Within 20 minutes, the strike force had dropped their ordnance and cleared the area, and the MiGs also stayed firmly on the ground at the remaining three airfields picked out for special attention by the 4th FW. No shots had been fired at any of the airfields as briefed, and the fighter-bombers returned to their bases unmolested by MiGs. This bold strategy had worked to perfection.

PROJECT *GUNVAL*

Against this background of increased MiG activity and ever-larger bases in Manchuria, elements of the 4th FW were involved in top-secret test project Operation *Gunval* in early January 1953, which involved the testing of 20 mm cannon fitted in seven specially modified F-86Fs. The wing itself had been flying conventionally armed F-models since September that year, and although the new variant's overall performance was significantly better than the F-86A/E, frustratingly for pilots flying the aircraft, its armament remained the same.

The 4th FW had regularly sent reports back to USAF HQ stating that more MiGs could have been destroyed had their Sabres been fitted with cannon rather than machine guns. F-86 pilots had quickly worked out that it was taking an estimated 1000 rounds to bring down one out of every three MiGs that were engaged. Worst still, there was gun camera film that showed over 1500 rounds hitting a MiG that continued to fly, and almost certainly made it safely back to its Manchurian base.

Stung into action by such criticism, the USAF instructed North American to swap the six 0.50-cal machine guns for four T-160 20 mm cannon in four F-86E-10s and six F-86F-1s as they were rolling down the production line – all were subsequently redesignated F-86F-2s. Thoroughly tested at Eglin and Edwards AFBs, eight of the jets were shipped to the Far East in December 1952 and seven duly issued to a select group of pilots from the 335th FS to evaluate in combat for 16 weeks from mid January.

The unit decided to operate the cannon-equipped Sabres in mixed formations with conventionally armed F-86s so that the communist pilots would struggle to pick out the modified jets. The killing power of the T-160 proved to be excellent when unleashed against the MiGs, as these weapons could fire at a much faster rate than the MiG-15's single N-37 37 mm and dual NS-23 23 mm cannon.

However, a serious problem was immediately encountered by the 335th FS within days of the evaluation starting. Gun gas was being ingested into the engine intake whenever the weapons were fired at high altitude, causing a compressor stall and engine flame-out. Two *Gunval*

Ace Capt Lonnie Moore of the 335th FS was one of just a handful of 4th FW pilots to regularly fly one of the seven Project *Gunval* F-86Fs based at Kimpo AB in the early months of 1953. The jet that bore his name was F-86F-2 51-2836, which is seen here marked with the 1.5 victory symbols following Moore's shared claim on 13 March and full kill on 12 April – the latter victory was the last to fall to the cannon-armed Sabres in Korea. This particular jet was one of two *Gunval* F-86Fs to suffer battle damage whilst fighting MiGs, although this was repaired at Kimpo AB prior to the Sabres being returned to the USA after the project had ended on 1 May 1953 (*Paul Peterson*)

All Korean War Sabre aces, and now F-86 instructors, this all-star line-up was photographed at Nellis AFB in late 1953. They are, from left to right, Capt Robert Moore (16th FS/51st FW, five kills), Capt Robert Latshaw (335th FS/4th FW, five kills), Maj William Whisner (25th FS/51st FW, 5.5 kills), Capt Iven Kincheloe (35th FS/51st FW, five kills) and, kneeling, Lt Col George Jones (4th and 51st FWs, 6.5 kills) (*John Henderson*)

jets were lost due to this problem before a solution was finally found.

One of the most experienced pilots to fly in this project was future 6.5-kill ace Lt Col George L Jones, who had previously claimed victories with both the 4th and 51st FWs in 1951-52. Formerly CO of the latter wing, he returned to Korea as leader of Project *Gunval*;

'Our jets were always blended in with standard 335th FS Sabres so as not to cause undue curiosity amongst the MiG pilots that they encountered. On one particular mission that I participated in, having launched from Kimpo, we passed through 15,000 ft and I kicked the rudder as the signal to spread out and test fire our guns. I squeezed off a quick burst of 20 mm rounds and watched the beeswax tracers slash out and converge through my gunsight. With our heads constantly on a swivel, we arrived over "MiG Alley" at noon at 42,000 ft on a beautiful day, with visibility unlimited. It was peaceful, which also made it seem a little "spooky".

'As was to be expected, suddenly a sizeable cloud of dust appeared over on the runway at Antung AB. This belonged to a large gaggle of MiG-15s that were preparing to get airborne and challenge the patrolling F-86s. The Sabre pilots were spread out, maintaining radio silence. To our advantage, we had more F-86s converging on the area, and they were about 50 miles out. They had been instructed to create as much attention as possible through radio chatter. Thanks to the MiG's superior rate of climb, it didn't take long for them to gain altitude – the first sightings were called out as "12 o'clock high".

'When their position was called out, we picked up numerous pinpoint flashes of light from the MiG canopies just like sun reflecting off of a mirror. These dots of light soon increased into an ominous view of many red-nose MiG-15s that were converging on our position. At that time, I broke radio silence, ordering "Drop tanks 'King Flight!'" Those external tanks tumbled end-over-end from eight miles up. I made sure my gunsight was switched on and the wingspan was set at 32 ft, which was the MiG's measurements. The orange dot and the diamonds glowed with reassuring brightness on the windscreen in front of me.

'The hostile gaggle was in a spread formation of twos, stacked up and back. The enemy formation had dropped down in altitude, and waggling my wings for the others to follow, I plunged down toward them at full throttle in the point position, which meant that my closure rate for a head-on attack was terrific. I rolled over the top of the last two MiGs into a gut-wrenching turn, and halfway around I slacked off a little on the Gs. I briefly caught a glimpse of two more enemy fighters coming in above us, and I called out for our second element to get them off of us!'

One of the most amazing things about a dogfight involving a large number of aircraft is that one second the sky is full and the next there is nothing in sight. In an effort to remain in visual contact with the low MiGs, yet still try to manoeuvre away from those coming in from altitude, Lt Col Jones and his wingman lost visual contact with all of the enemy jets, as well as his own second element. But knowing how many canopy reflections he had seen, he knew that there were still some MiGs close by, and he was right. Seconds later the radio crackled that more bogies had been sighted at '12 o'clock low', and Jones' element dove down to set up a firing pass;

'These two must have seen us because they went into a shallow high speed turn to the left. It was evident that these guys knew what they were doing, as they went into a steeper turn. It was easier for me to cut them off, so I told my wingman that I would take the bounce and he could cover me. By now they were very close to crossing north of the Yalu, and that was a strict no-no for us. I reasoned that it would be okay to pursue them for a very short distance into Manchuria, however. We had the altitude advantage at 45,000 ft, and our dive was closing the gap fast. Suddenly, the two MiGs split up, with one pulling up and to the right in an attempt to get above us. The other stayed on course. I told wing to keep an eye on the top one, as it appeared that they were setting up for a vertical scissors manoeuvre on us.

'Hoping to avoid a compressor stall when I fired my 20 mm cannon, I switched my gun control to two guns only. Picking up some speed from a shallow dive, I eased back on the stick and flew the sight onto the MiG's tailpipe. I was squarely in his jet wash, and my F-86 was jumping all over the place. This was also true for my gunsight, and in an effort to slow him down, I took a chance and fired a short burst. The rounds missed their mark, or at least I think they did! The MiG immediately jerked up and down like a yo-yo on a short string and then steadied out.

'Once again, I eased up on the throttle and pulled back in behind at 2000 ft, and that put me right back in his jet wash. Getting the sight squarely on him was impossible. We were at extreme altitude, and I knew that I was skating on thin air. One bad move and I could stall out.'

Not all dogfights end with a spectacular kill, and this proved to be one of them. Jones fired several bursts, scoring numerous hits on the MiG's

These four 335th FS Sabres are seen on the alert pad at Kimpo, each one being plugged into a generator for an instant engine start should the call come to scramble the alert flight. The pilots assigned to these aircraft would be sat somewhere nearby, fully suited up and ready to go. Fortunately, the scrambles that were performed by the 4th FW during the war rarely resulted in actual combat for the alert pilots (*USAF*)

4th FW CO Col James K Johnson used this F-86F-10 (51-12941) to claim most of his 11 kills, the aircraft being looked after by the 335th FS (*Harry Jones*)

Col James K Johnson stands up in the cockpit of 51-12941 for an official USAF combat portrait soon after returning from a mission in the spring of 1953 (*USAF*)

left wing. One final burst hit the wing in the same place as the first one and the jet slowed down considerably. This allowed the cannon-equipped Sabre to line up for the fatal burst, which ultimately never came.

At that very moment, the second MiG launched an attack on Jones' wingman and scored some major hits. It was his call for help that forced Jones to break off his attack against the heavily damaged MiG, and a certain kill.

When both men returned to base, they were amazed to see the damage inflicted to the wingman's Sabre. The MiG pilot had put one of his 37 mm rounds through the jet's fuselage right behind the cockpit, the round penetrating the aft self-sealing fuel tank. No leak showed, and because the aircraft was flying at such a high altitude, the fuel did not have a chance to burn. The MiG pilot had taken a 90-degree deflection shot at a 600 mph target from a high side approach at an altitude of 49,000 ft! Jones and his wingman were amazed, and they were left wondering whether the pilot had meant to do this, or had just taken a very lucky shot as he flashed past the Sabre?

Jones was given credit for a probable kill, and his gun camera film showed that, at a distance of only 1200 ft from the MiG, he had been just seconds away from a confirmed victory!

There was no doubting Jones' kill claim on 29 March 1953, when he achieved a spectacular head-on victory. His section encountered several flights of MiGs that were on a reciprocating course at about the same altitude over the Yalu. With Jones out in front, he fixed his gunsight on one of the converging fighters, despite a closure rate in excess of 1000 mph. Setting his firing reticule at 400 ft, he waited until the MiG literally filled his gunsight before opening fire. Jones had only a split-second to take a shot at the enemy jet before he had to release the trigger and nudge the stick over slightly as the formations raced passed each other in an out-of-focus blur.

Soon after they had crossed, Jones' flight came under attack from a different angle. After a gut-wrenching dive and some violent

manoeuvring, the MiGs broke away and crossed north of the river. Once the Sabres had formed up again, Jones received a radio call from one of the pilots in the other flight telling him that the MiG he had fired on had blown up just seconds after they had passed each other. It was a confirmed kill for Jones and the power-packed 20 mm cannon.

As previously mentioned, the only *Gunval* jets lost during the trial fell victim to engine flame-outs caused by gun gas ingestion. A number of other aircraft had close calls in combat with the hordes of MiG-15s over 'MiG Alley', and one *Gunval* pilot came within seconds of being shot down by a fellow 4th FW pilot. His exact identity was unknown at the time, as it could have been one of either three aces – Lt Col George L Jones, Col James K Johnson or Capt Lonnie Moore – that flew the cannon-armed jets during this period. As 334th FS pilot 1Lt Bruno Giordano recalled, the only thing that saved the ace was a small puff of smoke;

'This close call mission was flown during a period of particularly heavy MiG activity in March. I was flight leader at the time, and with so many experienced combat pilots in the 4th FW, it was unusual to have a lieutenant flying lead. The weather that day was absolutely beautiful, with almost unlimited visibility. 2Lt Joe Bryant was flying on my wing for the mission, and we were a little late in taking off from Kimpo. Regardless, we had no trouble on the way to "MiG Alley", and we entered the combat area at a high rate of speed, with full internal tanks and plenty of altitude. There were already F-86s involved in numerous dogfights up ahead, and we were coming in to relieve the ones that were getting low on fuel.

'There were a lot of MiGs in the area, and I could see several gaggles up ahead and below. It was very unusual to see them at a lower altitude, which meant that we had a good height advantage for once. I peeled off and went screaming down after them, trying to pick a target out to go after, but there were so many jets in the air that it was tough.

'I saw one of the swept-wing fighters open fire, its guns leaving "puffs" of smoke in its wake as the rounds left the jet. This caught my attention, because when an F-86 fired, the puffs were very close together due to the rapidity at which the 0.50-cal machine guns discharged their ordnance. Conversely, with the MiG-15's 23 mm and 37 mm cannon, there was a

335th FS pilot Capt Karl Dittmer shot down two MiG-15s in this Canadian-built F-86E-6(CAN) in the autumn of 1952. Aside from being an exceptional fighter pilot, he was also one of the most talented artists in the 4th FW. Indeed, he painted many of the names and nose arts seen on the Sabres at Kimpo during this period (*Karl Dittmer*)

Capt Manuel J Fernandez poses in his winter flying gear in early 1953. Listed as the 26th USAF jet ace of the Korean War with 14.5 kills, he shot down his fifth MiG-15 on 18 February and his last on 16 May 1953. Leaving the USAF in 1963, Fernandez worked in civil aviation until he was killed in a flying accident in October 1980 (*USAF*)

lot more space between the puffs because of the weapons' slower rate of fire.

'Anyway, when the aeroplane I was interested in fired, it was obviously not an F-86 due to the intervals between the "puffs", so I locked onto it and told 2Lt Bryant that I was going after it.

'I bore down on the "MiG" as he was bouncing off an attack on another aircraft. At the angle I was coming in on him, it was an absolute broadside shot for me. I had my pipper dead-on, and I was ready to blow him away, but fortunately I waited a few more seconds

to get closer to my target. About two seconds before I pulled the trigger, I saw that my   "target" had yellow stripes on the wings – I almost had a heart attack! It was an F-86 from our 4th FW. I berated myself for screwing up and   locking onto the wrong aircraft. By the time I pulled off of him and came back around, the sky was empty!

'Years later, I was having a drink in a bar in Tripoli with a fellow Korean War aviator, and we got to talking about the strange things that had happened during our years of flying. I mentioned this particular close shave, and my new-found pilot friend told me that "my" F-86 was being flown by ace Capt Lonnie Moore, who had come over to Korea on a top secret project that involved the testing of 20 mm cannon in the F-86F. That explained the intermittent puffs of smoke coming from his guns. He was just half a second away from being on the receiving end of a hail of 0.50-cal rounds.'

There are numerous kill symbols painted on the side of Capt Manuel Fernandez's final Sabre (F-86F-1 51-2857), with the 17 below the cockpit credited to him. Fernandez downed 14.5 MiGs, and damaged two more. The rest of these red stars denote claims made by other pilots that flew the jet following Fernandez's hasty return home in late May 1953 (*Bill Graski*)

ACE RACE

Whilst the *Gunval* evaluation was going on, 4th FW pilots flying conventionally armed Sabres continued to rack up the victories. Aside from Lt Col Jones, two more aces were crowned in February and March 1953. The first of these was Capt Manuel 'Pete' Fernandez, who claimed his fifth and sixth kills on 18 February.

Fernandez had enlisted in the Army Air Corps in World War 2 straight from high school, but his first operational assignment was in the Panama Canal Zone after the war. He became an instructor at Nellis AFB, and it

Capt Fernandez's F-86F-1 is seen in flight returning from a patrol up north. Although the pilot has punched off his external tanks in anticipation of MiG-related action, there is no tell-tale gun powder smudging around the nose to indicate that he has tangled with any communist jets on this particular flight. The Sabre has eight kill symbols just aft of the gun troughs (*USAF*)

soon became obvious he was a natural at air-to-air gunnery. In fact, his uncanny touch was partly due to natural ability, but also to constant practice on the ranges near Nellis. Fernandez's first encounter with a MiG was on 4 October 1952, and in a matter of seconds he had positioned his Sabre for the shot, fired two quick bursts and destroyed the target. The second kill resulted from one long burst and the third from two shorter ones – he would often return from a mission with ammunition left in the magazines of his guns.

When Fernandez fired he usually hit what he aimed at, and by the time his tour ended in mid May 1953, his tally stood at 14.5 kills. Only his great rival Maj James Jabara would better this score within the 4th FW.

On 28 March 1953, the wing's final wartime CO, Col James K Johnson, bagged a MiG to give him ace status, the World War 2 veteran finishing his tour with ten communist jets to his credit.

During the final months of the war, the USAF's score of MiGs increased significantly. There were several reasons for this, with the primary one being the greater number of MiG-15s in-theatre as a result of the enemy having stepped up its training programme in late 1952.

Both sides knew that the end of the war was months rather than years away, and because the conflict represented the best training ground for combat pilots, the pipeline was jammed. And, as recently-disclosed information shows, the Soviet presence had diminished somewhat since 1950-51. Therefore, by the early months of 1953, less skillful Chinese pilots, and perhaps North Koreans too, manned most MiG-15 regiments involved in the aerial fighting.

Statistics tell the story. Sabre pilots scored 99 kills in the first three months of 1953, yet the war's final quarter saw 170 MiGs destroyed. The 4th FW can take credit for many of these victories, with a handful of pilots claiming the vast percentage of the kills. The wing's two leading lights in the 'ace race' which developed in 1953 were 334th FS pilots Maj Jabara and Capt Fernandez, who between them were credited with 20.5 kills between January and July.

Five new aces were also produced by the wing in the high-scoring months of June and July, and three of them – Maj Vermont Garrison and Capts Lonnie Moore and Ralph Parr – finished the war with ten kills apiece.

Moore had been particularly prolific in early June, with his 1.5 kills claimed during a late afternoon 'MiG Alley' sweep on the 5th of the month having great significance, as

Maj James Jabara poses for the 4th FW photographer after achieving the status of double ace on 10 June 1953. The USAF's first jet ace, he would finish his second combat tour in Korea with a total of 15 kills to his credit. Post-war, Jabara became the youngest full colonel in the USAF at just 43 years of age when he was given command of the F-100 Super Sabre-equipped 31st TFW in 1966. Slated for a combat tour in Vietnam, Jabara perished in a car accident on 17 November 1966. His daughter, who was at the wheel of the vehicle, was also killed, and they were subsequently buried together in a single grave at Arlington Cemetery (*USAF*)

75

CO of the 335th FS, and a 7.333-kill ace from World War War 2 (again with the 4th FG), Maj Vermont Garrison was one of the most experienced combat pilots at Kimpo AB in the final year of the war. He claimed ten kills in Korea, with most of them being scored in this F-86F-10 (51-12953) (*Norman Green*)

Maj James Jabara's scoreboard on F-86F-30 52-4513 is seen in close up near the end of his second combat tour. Note the D- and P-adorned stars, denoting damaged and probable claims (*Larry Hendel*)

one of them was possibly the 700th MiG destroyed by F-86s in Korea. He and his wingman, 2Lt William F Schrimsher, claimed kills within 90 seconds of each other, and these were listed as the 699th and 700th kills in a Public Information Office/HQ Fifth Air Force press release issued the following day that also stated;

'Fifth Air Force Sabre jets have cost the Chinese and North Korean communists at least $140,000,000 in destroyed MiG-15s since December 1950. The exact cost of the Russian-built jet is unknown, but it is assumed that the cost is substantially less than that of the F-86 Sabre, whose cost averages about $272,913 per copy. Cheaper labour costs and considerably less electronic equipment would probably place the cost of the MiG-15 near $200,000 each.'

Aside from the 700 MiGs destroyed, 114 had probably been destroyed and 734 damaged. The press release also stated that 56 Sabres had been shot down by MiG-15s from December 1950 through to June 1953.

Moore and Schrimsher were part of a 335th FS patrol consisting of a flight of four aircraft made up of some of the best pilots in the unit. Flight lead was World War 2 ace Maj Vermont Garrison, who would claim his fifth and sixth MiGs during the mission, and on his wing was 1Lt Harry A Jones (he too got a MiG in this clash). The second element consisted of Capt Moore and 2Lt Schrimsher, and the latter recalled;

'We were well north of the Yalu River, which was a real no-no, but we did it on a fairly regular basis. Cruising at 40,000+ ft, Maj Garrison saw sun flashes down low, so we did a "Split-S" and headed down to the deck. What he had seen were several MiG-15s taking off from Antung. They were just above the mountain tops and climbing out at a low speed.

'Being No 4, I was a bit behind the rest of the flight, and our overtake speed was pretty high – I think we may have popped our speed brakes.

Garrison shot down two of them in quick succession, Jones destroyed one and Moore also scored. I started firing at one of the others, and he went into a hard break, snapped out of control and hit the side of a mountain. I had not hit him on that first burst, but I was credited with the kill. To my knowledge, it was the only time in the Korean War that all four pilots from a single flight were credited with at least one kill apiece. We downed five MiGs in total.

'I am sure that I got the 700th MiG of the war because I was flying in the No 4 slot, and was therefore the last one in the flight to get a kill.

'Regardless of whether this is true or not, I flew on the wing of some of the best shooters in Korea, especially Maj Vermont Garrison. He was one of the war's most aggressive Sabre pilots, and also one of the best. I saw far more action than most wingmen did. Years later, while I was at Moody AFB, in Georgia, Col Garrison came in to attend a conference. There, he paid me the greatest compliment I have ever gotten. He told the group that I was the best wingman that he ever flew with.'

Flying on Maj Garrison's wing on 5 June was 1Lt Harry A Jones, who claimed the flight's third victory;

'My primary job was protecting our flight lead, but things really heated up when we dove down into the gaggle of MiGs. Maj Garrison got two kills pretty quickly, and right after that we were at 5000 ft in the general vicinity of the Suiho Dam, which was located on the river. There were MiGs all over the place, and I pulled up behind one of them and fired a long burst. The tracers showed that I was right on the mark, and he went into a half roll towards the deck. I followed right behind him, firing all the way and getting more good hits. Just before he hit the ground, I thought I saw the canopy blow, but a split-second later the MiG exploded on impact. I don't think that the pilot had a chance to eject. We were at a very low altitude when the fight started.'

The remaining pilot in that flight was Capt Lonnie Moore, and he was probably the one to bag the fourth MiG of the mission (699th of the war). During the subsequent debriefing back at Kimpo AB, he gave an account of what he remembered of the melee;

Having finished his mission briefing, Lt Col Vermont Garrison has suited up and been driven out to his jet on the 335th FS ramp. With his preflight walkaround check of his jet complete, he is seen in the throes of climbing into his Sabre prior to flying another combat air patrol over 'MiG Alley' (*Bill Graski*)

335th FS pilot Capt Clyde Curtin became the 38th Sabre ace of the war on 19 July 1953 with a double MiG haul in this very F-86F-30 (52-4416), which he had christened *Boomer* (*Bert Beecroft*)

Also seen on page 29, F-86E-10 51-2824 of the 336th FS was used by Maj Stephen Bettinger to 'make ace' on 20 July 1953, although it was then shot down by another MiG-15. It was one of six Sabres lost in combat on this date. Although the *Bugs Bunny* artwork seen in this photograph is identical to the marking worn by the jet on page 29, note that the aircraft has had its 336th FS rocket badge removed (*Dick Hintermeier*)

'We caught several MiGs down at a very low altitude today. I locked on to one that was down around 1000 ft, and with my Sabre in a diving attitude, I was able to run up close behind him and almost overran him. One long burst into the wing and tail section caused an explosion within the jet's fuselage, which in turn started to burn fiercely.

'All of our flight's kills today were claimed at low altitude, and every one of the MiGs we attacked exploded. I think that this had something to do with how low we were. Usually, kills made up at 40,000 ft or so don't seem to burn like these did. I got to within 500 ft of the rear of my MiG before I squeezed the trigger. When I finished firing, I pulled on up alongside him and could see a large hole in his fuselage and fire burning inside his tailpipe. It appeared that the entire insides of the MiG were being consumed by fire. Right before it plummeted the short distance to the ground, I saw the pilot get out.'

Fittingly, having been the pioneer Sabre group in-theatre, the 4th FW had the honour of securing the last two F-86 aces credited with five kills during the Korean War. Capt Clyde Curtin of the 335th FS downed his fifth victory on 19 July and the 336th FS's Maj Stephen Bettinger got his the following day, although the latter pilot was then downed by a second MiG-15 moments later and captured by the Chinese.

The final MiG-15 kill of the Korean War fell to 2Lt Sam Young of the 51st FW's 25th FS on 22 July 1953. For the next five days the communist fighters did not venture much into harm's way south of the Yalu. Indeed, for 48 hours between the 23rd and the 25th, the weather was so bad over much of Korea that neither side took to the skies. With the ceasefire expected to be announced at any time, pilots from both the 4th and 51st FW's were itching to register the war's final victory, and on the 27th 335th FS ace Capt Ralph S Parr achieved this feat.

With the weather having cleared overnight, on the 27th the Sabres were up in force. Following a three-day lull in the action, the odds of it being a big day for MiG activity seemed very good. Capt Parr and his wingman were flying escort duty up in the Chunggangjin area when the ace sighted a conventional transport type he identified as a Soviet-built Ilyushin Il-12, complete with red stars on its wings and fuselage.

Making two passes on the aircraft to make sure there was no mistake, Parr confirmed that it was indeed hostile and fired a long burst into it. Seconds later the Il-12 exploded. It was the last confirmed aerial kill of the Korean War, and it gave Parr double ace status.

DOUBLE ACES

Ralph Parr was the last of 11 Sabre pilots to claim ten or more kills in Korea, and no fewer than nine of these aviators hailed from the 4th FW.

As with previous aerial conflicts, F-86 pilots needed skill, luck and, above all, aggressiveness to attain ace status. A veteran of the final months of the Pacific War, as well as 165 combat missions in F-80s in Korea in 1950-51, Capt Parr exhibited all these attributes when he claimed his first two kills on 7 June 1953.

This mission involved a flight of 335th FS Sabres, call-sign 'John Shark' flight, that was on a routine combat patrol over 'MiG Alley'. The flight had commenced its sweep at 43,000 ft, flying 20 miles south of, and parallel to, the Yalu River. The lead jet was flown by 1Lt Merton E Ricker, with Col Robert Dixon in the No 2 slot. The second element was led by 2Lt Al B Cox (No 3), whilst his wingman was Capt Ralph Parr (No 4), who had only just joined the squadron. The weather was CAVU (ceiling and visibility unlimited) – perfect for hunting MiGs.

The fighters' GCI had the call-sign 'Romeo', and it was not long before 1Lt Ricker heard the controller calling 'Bandit tracks' over his radio. Upon hearing this, Ricker called for the flight to jettison external tanks.

On their second swing to the northeast, Capt Parr spotted a flight of MiGs climbing towards them at an incredible closure rate from their left side. He immediately called out, '"John Shark", break left. MiGs close and firing!' Fortunately, the MiGs came in from 90 degrees off and flew straight through the Sabre flight without scoring any hits. 1Lt Ricker and his wingman pursued the fleeing jets, but the latter had a tremendous speed advantage.

By this time the Sabres were getting close to 'bingo' fuel, and Ricker, still chasing the MiGs, radioed that all of them should start preparing to head back to base. 2Lt Cox decided to complete one final orbit as he led Parr back up to 41,000 ft following their loss of height evading the MiGs' 'hit and run' attack.

Whilst climbing, Capt Parr glanced down to his right in the direction of the Yalu and spotted movement near to the ground. Struggling to break out the contact, Cox told Parr to take the lead whilst he covered him – during the pre-mission briefing that morning, Cox had confirmed to Parr that if he called out any bogies that he in turn could not see, the wingman was cleared to initiate the fight. And with his previous combat experience to draw on, Parr was well qualified to take the bounce.

Rolling over and entering a 'Split-S' manoeuvre with full power, Parr headed straight down in a southwesterly direction. Seeing his wingman

Wearing his flying gear, 335th FS double ace Capt Ralph S Parr strikes a familiar pose for his official photograph. The 33rd pilot to become a Sabre ace, he finished his tour with exactly ten kills (and three damaged) to his credit (*USAF*)

Vice-President of the United States Richard M Nixon gets some first hand information on how an F-86 works by Capt Ralph Parr whilst visiting the troops in Korea in the spring of 1953 (*Dick Erratt*)

roll over towards him, Cox entered a right banking turn in an effort to keep his eyes firmly locked onto the plummeting Sabre as it crossed under him. However, because Parr was in a steep nose-dive, it took just seconds for him to completely disappear from Cox's view. The latter immediately radioed Parr to find out where he was, and he received the curt reply 'Straight down. Come on down and find me!' It was obvious that he was concentrating totally on the MiGs at hand.

Levelling off at less than 200 ft, and pulling maximum Gs, Parr closed in behind the MiG that he had spotted. But instead of one, there were two, and suddenly there were four, then eight. By then it was too late for Parr to back off, so he pressed home his attack just as two more flights (eight MiGs) came into view. He had run up against 16 MiG-15s, and he was all alone! With no way to escape, Parr closed to within 3000 ft of the lead jet, and just as he was about to open fire, the entire gaggle of enemy fighters broke in every direction except down! Parr pulled the throttle back to idle and popped his speed brakes to keep from overshooting. He then pulled the trigger, and the sharp curve of the tracers and the slowing rate of fire got his attention – he was pulling over 9 Gs. The gunsight fuse blew at 9+ G, further adding to his problems!

Capt Parr recalled what happened next;

'After slowly overshooting, I watched the MiG leader reverse until we were literally canopy-to-canopy in a rolling scissors, with each of us looking into the other's cockpit. I waited for an opportunity, and it came when the MiG pilot made a slight change. With a little forward stick and some rudder, I slid in behind him so close that I thought I would hit him with the nose of my Sabre. I backed off just a bit and was still at pointblank range, which was about ten feet. We were still right down on the deck too! Gunsight or no gunsight, I could not miss, but each time I fired, my aircraft would stall out due to the extremely tight turn and the vibration of the guns. My only option was to work my way through the MiG's jet wash and into position again.

These five Sabre pilots shot down no fewer than 55 enemy aircraft between them whilst flying with the 4th FW in Korea. They are, from left to right, Capt Lonnie Moore (10 kills), Lt Col Vermont Garrison (10 kills), Col James K Johnson (10 kills), Capt Ralph Parr (10 kills) and Maj James Jabara (15 kills). This photograph was taken at Kimpo AB in early June 1953, with Col Johnson's Sabre providing the backdrop (*Bill Graski*)

'By the time I had fired my fourth or fifth burst, my F-86 was soaked with MiG fuel. My next burst resulted in flames streaming from the MiG back around both sides of my aircraft and over the canopy. At that moment the communist fighter's engine quit and I shot past it just as the jet nosed into the ground and exploded.

'But the action was far from over at this point, as another MiG was closing on me from the left. An immediate overshoot allowed me to reverse and, firing a long burst straight ahead, the tracers walked right through the MiG before it could get out of range.'

Now there were five MiGs trying to cut inside, and Parr had to pull a tight left turn to keep them at bay. All of this was playing out at almost treetop level, and he was firing at anything that popped up in front of him. Evidently, Parr got one MiG pilot's attention, because when he tried to manoeuvre out of the Sabre's line of fire, his jet hit the ground and exploded. Moments later the remaining MiGs broke off and headed back toward the Yalu. About the same time, 1Lt Cox found Parr and joined up with him. Both F-86s were very low on fuel, but they made it safely back to base. Despite taking on 16 MiG-15s in a low, twisting dogfight at close quarters, Parr and his Sabre had emerged totally unscathed with two destroyed and one damaged to their credit.

Capt Parr's record in Korea was nothing short of outstanding, as all ten of his kills were achieved within the span of just 30 missions during the final seven weeks of the war.

81

Combat Chronology for the 4th FW in Korea

15 November 1950
Some 49 F-86As and 200 airmen arrived at NAS North Island, San Diego. The aircraft would be placed on the carrier USS *Cape Esperance* for transportation to Japan. Many of the wing's personnel would make the trip on accompanying tankers, along with aircraft from the 336th FS. This move was the direct result of Eastern Air Defense Force warning order No 28-50, dated 9 November 1950

29 November 1950
Cape Esperance departed San Diego and arrived in Yokosuka, Japan, on 13 December with 334th and 335th FS Sabres on board

13 December 1950
Group CO Lt Col John C Meyer took an advanced detachment of 336th FS Sabres from Johnson AB, Japan, to Kimpo AB, Korea, and from there made the first orientation flights

17 December 1950
336th FS CO Lt Col Bruce Hinton spotted four MiG-15s just south of the Yalu River at 32,000 ft. His flight dropped tanks and dived down on them, Hinton firing 1500 rounds at the leader's wingman. The enemy aircraft crashed and burned. The remaining three MiGs escaped by accelerating away from the F-86s. Hinton claimed the Sabre's premier MiG kill during the USAF fighter's first combat mission

22 December 1950
While cruising at 35,000 ft, eight F-86As encountered four MiG-15s and lost one of their number in the fight that ensued. Later that day, eight more Sabres tangled with fifteen MiGs. Functioning with textbook precision, Lt Col John C Meyer, leading one flight, got one MiG, while Lt Col Glenn T Eagleston, leading the other flight, got another, with various other members of the flight accounting for four more between them without loss. This was the first major all-jet engagement in history

30 December 1950
4th FW had flown 234 sorties in December, of which 76 had seen MiG engagements. The results were eight confirmed kills and two probables for the loss of one F-86

6 March 1951
334th FS began staging patrols from Suwon AB, even

though its single concrete runway was surrounded by mud. The squadron permanently moved into Suwon on 10 March

12 April 1951
Some 39 B-29s, escorted by F-84s, and with F-86s flying high cover, were attacked by more than 70 MiGs while they were bombing the Sinuiju railway bridge. The F-86s shot down four MiGs and the B-29 gunners got six

20 April 1951
Future ranking ace of the 4th FW, Capt James Jabara, scored a MiG-15 kill to take his tally to four victories, thus setting him up to become the USAF's first jet ace one month later

22 April 1951
Twelve Sabres, low on fuel and beginning to head back to base, were jumped by 36 MiGs. Twelve fresh F-86s arrived to relieve the patrol. They immediately waded into the MiG formation and shot down four and damaged another four

1 May 1951
The 335th FS, flying in from Japan, relieved the 334th FS at Suwon AB. The latter unit in turn flew back to Johnson AB for R&R

20 May 1951
A big fight began brewing when about 50 MiGs came south of the river and were greeted by 36 Sabres. Despite the failure of one of his drop tanks to release, 334th FS pilot Capt Jabara, flying with the 335th FS, dove into the fight and shot down two MiGs to become the USAF's first jet ace

31 May 1951
No F-86s had officially been lost in action while they accomplished 3550 sorties and claimed 22 victories in the first five months of 1951. This record indicated the quality of the 4th FW's aircraft, pilots and maintenance crews

17 June 1951
At 0130 hrs a NKPAF Polikarpov Po-2 biplane snuck in at low altitude over Suwon and dropped two 25-lb fragmentation bombs on the 335th FS's dispersal area. One Sabre was destroyed and eight others damaged. This was the first of what soon became dubbed 'Bed-Check Charlie' attacks during the conflict

28 June 1951

Group CO, and World War 2 ace, Lt Col Glenn Eagleston came close to being shot down when his F-86 was hit by cannon fire from a MiG. A 37 mm shell exploded against the breech of the middle gun on the Sabre's port side and two 23 mm rounds hit the fuselage further back. His jet lurched out of control as it dropped to 15,000 ft, where Eagleston levelled it off and nursed the F-86 back to base. The aircraft had suffered major damage, proving the lethality of the MiG's firepower and the ruggedness of the Sabre

11 July 1951

When a large formation of F-80s was jumped by 30 MiGs south of the Yalu River, the communist fighters were in turn set upon by 34 Sabres patrolling in the area. Three MiGs were shot down without loss to the 4th FW

9 September 1951

No fewer than 70 MiGs attacked 22 Sabres in a wild dogfight. 1Lts Richard S Becker and Ralph D Gibson each claimed a kill to become the USAF's second and third jets aces of the war

16 October 1951

A total of nine MiG-15s were shot down without loss to the 4th FW during the course of two big dogfights over 'MiG Alley'. This was the highest score yet for any one day in the war

23 October 1951

Eight B-29s en route to bomb a major North Korean airfield were set upon by around 150 MiG-15s – the largest display of communist jet activity to date. The bombers were escorted by 55 F-84s and 34 Sabres, the latter flying top cover. While 100 MiGs kept the Sabres tied up, 50 more penetrated the F-84 formations to get at the bombers. Within minutes, three B-29s and one F-84 had been shot down, with four more bombers being badly mauled. In turn, the B-29 gunners downed three MiGs, the Sabres two and one fell to a Thunderjet. This mission, dubbed 'Black Tuesday', ended all B-29 daylight raids over North Korea

13 November 1951

Another big effort by the MiGs saw 50 Sabres tangle with 100+ MiGs in two different aerial battles. Twelve MiGs were shot down, with another one probably destroyed and three damaged. No Sabres were lost

27 November 1951

Maj Richard D Creighton of the 336th FS claimed his fifth MiG kill to become the fourth Sabre ace of the war

30 November 1951

A formation of 31 Sabres northbound from Suwon intercepted 12 Tu-2 twin-engined bombers, escorted by 16 La-9 piston-engined fighters, with 16 MiG-15s flying top cover. Eight Tu-2s, three La-9s and a MiG were shot down, while two F-86s were damaged. 334th FS CO Maj George A Davis claimed three Tu-2s destroyed and had to turn away from three others when his fuel became critically low. Suddenly, he found himself behind and below an unsuspecting MiG, and he shot it down to become the fifth Sabre ace of the war. 335th FS CO Maj Winton W Marshall became the sixth Sabre ace minutes after Davis when he downed a Tu-2 and a La-9 during this encounter

1 December 1951

The 51st FW at Suwon AB was declared operational with F-86Es on this date, the unit offering the 4th FW much-needed support as MiG ranks continued to grow unabated north of the Yalu River. The wing would initially be commanded by World War 2 ace Col Francis S Gabreski

13 December 1951

This proved to be the best day of the war for the 4th FW in respect to kills achieved, as 13 of the 145 MiGs seen were shot down. Four were credited to Maj George Davis, making him the first double ace of the war. The overall score for the month of December was 28 MiGs shot down by the 4th and 51st FWs for the loss of seven Sabres

17 December 1951

The Pentagon announced that the 4th FW had destroyed 130 Russian-built MiG-15s in combat to date. Its pilots had also claimed 20 probables and 144 damaged. A total of 14 Sabres had been lost

4 February 1952

Large formations of MiG-15s were sighted at altitudes exceeding 53,000 ft, which continued to put them out of reach for any F-86A pilots. This fact was reflected in that month's kill total for the wing of just six

10 February 1952

Maj George Davis was shot down and killed whilst attempting to come to the aid of F-84 Thunderjet fighter-bombers that were in trouble. He claimed his 13th and 14th kills before a MiG got on his tail and shot a wing off his jet. Davis was later awarded a posthumous Medal of Honor

March 1952

The total number of kills racked up by the 4th FW for this month was 25 MiGs (of 39 credited to both Sabre wings) for the loss of only three F-86s

13 April 1952

Sabre pilots from the 4th FW reported seeing between 400 and 500 MiG-15s parked at Ta-tungkou airfield. This was the highest number of enemy fighters ever observed on a single base in Manchuria

21 April 1952
Capt Robert J Love of the 335th FS shot down his fourth and fifth MiG-15s on the same mission to become the 11th Sabre ace of the war

3 May 1952
Capt Robert T Latshaw of the 335th FS claimed his fifth MiG to become the 14th F-86 ace of the war

13 May 1952
The 4th FW loaded 1000-lb bombs onto a number of its Sabres and sent them to bomb the airfield at Sinuiju. With dive brakes open, they hit the airfield before enemy gunners realised what was happening. A second group of Sabres attacked the Kumu-ri railway yards with their bombs, and group CO, and World War 2 ace, Col Walker H Mahurin was shot down and captured. He would remain a PoW until September 1953

15 May 1952
335th FS pilot 1Lt James H Kasler shot down two MiG-15s over 'MiG Alley' for his fourth and fifth kills, making him the 15th Sabre ace of the war

20 May 1952
The wing achieved another milestone when its CO, and World War 2 ace, Col Harrison R Thyng, shot down his fifth MiG-15 on a patrol close to the Yalu River to become the 16th Sabre ace of the war. His fourth kill had been claimed a month earlier on 18 April

June 1952
Having suffered heavy losses during the previous three months, the MiG units dramatically scaled back their air activity during June. Only 20 communist aircraft were shot down for the loss of four Sabres. However, the number of MiGs parked at several bases in Manchuria continued to increase

15 June 1952
2Lt James F Low bagged his fifth MiG to become the 17th Sabre ace of the war. His four confirmed victories in June gave him 20 per cent of all the kills scored by Sabre pilots for the month

July 1952
After a gradual changeover to the newer F-86E (the wing had received its first examples in the autumn of 1951), the 4th FW got rid of its last F-86A during July. This put the unit on an even par with the 51st FW, which had been exclusively equipped with E-models since converting from the F-80C in late 1951

1-8 August 1952
The relative lull in MiG activity over the previous two months ended during the first week of August when numerous dogfights with aggressively flown communist jets over 'MiG Alley' resulted in 17 enemy fighters being destroyed by the 4th FW for the loss of just one F-86

8 August 1952
Capt Clifford D Jolley of the 335th FS shot down his fifth MiG to become the 18th Sabre ace of the war. He would finish his tour with seven confirmed kills

4 September 1952
Maj Frederick C 'Boots' Blesse of the 334th FS shot down his fourth MiG-15, which made him an ace when these victories were combined with a La-9 that he had shot down on 20 June. Remaining with the wing for another month, he finished his tour as a double ace with ten kills

21 September 1952
Capt Robinson Risner of the 336th FS shot down his fourth and fifth MiG-15s on this date to become the 20th jet ace. He would claim three more victories by the end of his tour. 334th FS pilot 1Lt Charles Cleveland also claimed a MiG-15 destroyed on this date, but it was only accorded probable status. He would have to wait until 11 April 2000 for it to be confirmed, thus allowing him to become the Korean War's 40th Sabre ace

September 1952
Some 64 MiG-15s were downed in September by the 4th and 51st FWs, this being the second-highest kill tally month of the war. The 4th was credited with 37 of these victories

1 November 1952
Group CO Col Royal N Baker scored his fourth aerial victory on this date, which was also officially recognised as the 4th FW's 300th MiG kill. Baker would finish his combat tour with 12 MiGs and a solitary La-9 to his credit, these kills being claimed whilst flying with both the 335th and 336th FSs. This tally placed him fifth in the list of Sabre aces

11 November 1952
Col Baker shot down his fifth enemy aircraft to become the 21st jet ace

18 November 1952
334th FS pilot Capt Leonard W Lilley claimed his fifth kill on this date to become the 22nd Sabre ace. His total would reach seven by the end of his combat tour

18 February 1953
In a dogfight involving large numbers of MiG-15s and

F-86s, Capt Manuel J 'Pete' Fernandez of the 334th FS claimed two kills for his fifth and sixth victories. This haul made him the war's 26th Sabre ace

28 March 1953
Col James K Johnson, CO of the 4th FW, shot down a MiG-15 whilst flying with the 335th FS to take his victory tally to 5.5 kills. The 29th Sabre ace of the war, he would claim his tenth, and last, victory on 30 June

29 March 1953
Lt Col George L Jones had one of the lengthiest and most successful tours in Korea of all the Sabre pilots to see action, and he became the 30th jet ace on this date. His first 1.5 kills were claimed with the 4th FW in late 1951, soon after which he transferred to the 51st FW to help Col Gabreski get the wing ready for combat operations. Shooting down two more MiG-15s whilst leading the 51st in January 1952, Jones was posted home three months later. Given command of Project *Gunval*, he returned to the 4th FW in January 1953 and flew combat missions with the 335th FS in cannon-armed F-86Fs. Jones's final four kill claims (two and two shared victories) were achieved in *Gunval* Sabres between 13 January and 7 April 1953

16 May 1953
Capt 'Pete' Fernandez scored his final victory on this date to take his tally to 14.5 kills, giving him a brief lead in the 'ace race'. Publicity surrounding this victory was Fernandez's undoing, however, as FEAF HQ discovered that he had flown 125 missions, which was 25 more than he was supposed to! He was immediately grounded and sent home. Fernandez would finish the war as its third ranking Sabre ace. That same day Maj James Jabara claimed his first kill (and his seventh overall) since returning to action with the 334th FS in January 1953

16 May 1953
A large number of MiG-15s came down from their high altitude perch and tangled with the F-86s. Pilots from the 4th FW shot down 11 and damaged six for the loss of just one Sabre

18 May 1953
Capt Fernandez's lead in the 'ace race' was ended when the 51st FW's ranking ace, Capt Joseph McConnell of the 39th FS, was credited with three kills, raising his final total to 16 victories. He was immediately ordered to stand down and return home, having flown 106 missions. McConnell was the top-scoring F-86 pilot of the Korean War, and one of only two triple aces to fly the Sabre

5 June 1953
Maj Vermont Garrison, flying with the 335th FS, scored

two kills to take his tally to six overall. This made him the 32nd Sabre ace. Before his tour was up, he would be promoted to lieutenant colonel and be credited with ten MiG-15s shot down

7 June 1953
Thirty-six Sabres from the 4th FW flew top cover for a maximum effort attack on the Sui-ho Dam by F-84 fighter-bombers. During the course of the mission, future double ace Capt Ralph Parr shot down two MiG-15s for his first kills of the war

18 June 1953
335th FS pilot Capt Lonnie R Moore scored his fifth kill to put himself in the record books as the 33rd F-86 ace. During the same mission squadronmate Capt Ralph Parr destroyed two MiG-15s, which made him the 34th Sabre ace. It was his second double-kill mission in 11 days, and like Moore, he would finish the war as a double ace with ten victories

June 1953
This was the highest scoring month of the war for the Sabres, with 78 MiG-15s being confirmed as destroyed. Some 44 of these were credited to the 4th FW

15 July 1953
Maj James Jabara claimed his 15th, and last, kill, after which he was immediately declared tour-expired by FEAF HQ. His tally would not be bettered in the 4th FW, and he became only the second Sabre triple ace of the war

19 July 1953
Capt Clyde A Curtin shot down two MiG-15s for his fourth and fifth victories. The 335th FS pilot became the 38th Sabre ace in the process

20 July 1953
With only one week left in the war, Maj Stephen L Bettinger of the 336th FS shot down his fifth MiG-15 to become the 39th, and last, jet ace officially recognised as such during the Korean War. Minutes later he was shot down by a MiG-15 and made a PoW. He was later repatriated as part of Operation *Big Switch*

27 July 1953
This proved to be the last day of the war, and there was a maximum effort put in by every UN aircraft type until last light in order to prevent last minute gains by communist forces. Capt Ralph S Parr shot down an Il-12 transport at 1230 hrs for the final aerial victory of the 37-month war. This controversial kill (the USSR claimed that the Ilyushin was a civil airliner shot down over Manchuria, rather than a military transport intercepted over North Korea) elevated him to the status of double ace

Aces of the 4th FW (In Order of Achieving Ace Status)

Capt James Jabara (1st jet ace of the war)
*** 1.5 confirmed kills in World War 2
334th FS
Total kills – 15 (scored over two combat tours)
First kill on 3 April 1951
Final kill on 15 July 1953

1Lt Richard S Becker (2nd jet ace of the war)
334th FS
Total kills – 5
First kill on 22 April 1951
Final kill on 9 September 1951

1Lt Ralph D Gibson (3rd jet ace of the war)
335th FS
Total kills – 5
First kill on 18 June 1951
Final kill on 9 September 1951

Maj Richard D Creighton (4th jet ace of the war)
*** 2 kills in World War 2
336th FS
Total kills – 7
First kill on 18 June 1951
Final kill on 27 November 1951

Maj George A Davis (5th jet ace of the war)
*** 7 confirmed kills in World War 2
334th FS Commanding Officer
Total kills – 14
First kill on 27 November 1951
Final kill on 10 February 1952

Maj Winton W Marshall (6th jet ace of the war)
335th FS Commanding Officer
Total kills – 6.5
First kill on 1 September 1951
Final kill on 5 December 1951

Capt Robert J Love (11th jet ace of the war)
335th FS
Total kills – 6
First kill on 20 March 1952
Final kill on 3 May 1952

Capt Robert T Latshaw (14th jet ace of the war)
335th FS
Total kills – 5
First kill on 25 January 1952
Final kill on 3 May 1952

1Lt James H Kasler (15th jet ace of the war)
335th FS
Total kills – 6
First kill on 1 April 1952
Final kill on 25 May 1952

Col Harrison R Thyng (16th jet ace of the war)
*** 5 confirmed kills in World War 2
4th FW Commanding Officer
Total kills – 5
First kill on 25 October 1951
Final kill on 20 May 1952

2Lt James F Low (17th jet ace of the war)
335th FS
Total kills – 9
First kill on 8 May 1952
Final kill on 18 December 1952

Capt Clifford D Jolley (18th jet ace of the war)
335th FS
Total kills – 7
First kill on 4 May 1952
Final kill on 11 October 1952

Maj Frederick C Blesse (19th jet ace of the war)
334th FS
Total kills – 10
First kill on 25 May 1952
Final kill on 3 October 1952

Capt Robinson Risner (20th jet ace of the war)
336th FS
Total kills – 8
First kill on 5 August 1952
Final kill on 21 January 1953

Col Royal N Baker (21st jet ace of the war)
*** 3.5 confirmed kills in World War 2
4th FG Commanding Officer
Total kills – 13
First kill on 20 June 1952
Final kill on 13 March 1953

Capt Leonard W Lilley (22nd jet ace of the war)
334th FS
Total kills – 7
First kill on 30 August 1952
Final kill on 14 January 1953

Capt Manuel J Fernandez (27th jet ace of the war)
334th FS
Total kills – 14.5
First kill on 4 October 1952
Final kill on 16 May 1953

Col James K Johnson (29th jet ace of the war)
*** 1 confirmed kill in World War 2
4th FG Commanding Officer
Total kills – 10
First kill on 13 January 1953
Final Kill on 30 June 1953

Lt Col George L Jones (30th jet ace of the war)
4th FW HQ (1.5 kills)/51st FW (2 kills)/335th FS (3 kills)
Total kills – 6.5
First kill on 1 October 1951
Final kill on 7 April 1953

Maj Vermont Garrison (32nd jet ace of the war)
*** 7.333 confirmed kills in World War 2
335th FS Commanding Officer
Total kills – 10
First kill on 21 February 1953
Final kill on 19 July 1953

Capt Lonnie R Moore (33rd jet ace of the war)
335th FS
Total kills – 10
First kill on 13 March 1953
Final kill on 19 July 1953

Capt Ralph S Parr (34th jet ace of the war)
335th FS
Total kills – 10
First kill on 7 June 1953
Final kill on 27 July 1953

Capt Clyde A Curtin (38th jet ace of the war)
335th FS
Total kills – 5
First kill on 11 October 1952
Final kill on 19 July 1953

Maj Stephen L Bettinger (39th jet ace of the war)
*** 1 confirmed kill in World War 2
336th FS
Total kills – 5
First Kill on 5 June 1953
Final kill on 20 July 1953

1Lt Charles G Cleveland (40th jet ace of the war*)
334th FS
Total kills – 5
First kill on 5 August 1952
Fourth kill on 28 September 1952
* Probable claim on 21 September 1952 upgraded to a
confirmed kill in 4/2000

Capt Brooks Liles
*** 1 confirmed kill in World War 2
336th FS
Total kills – 4 (plus 1 in World War 2 to give him ace
status)
First kill on 21 February 1952
Fourth kill on 21 April 1952

Capt Conrad Mattson
*** 1 confirmed kill in World War 2
334th FS
Total kills – 4 (plus 1 in World War 2 to give him ace
status)
First kill on 11 March 1952
Fourth kill on 30 April 1952

4th FW's Overall Aerial Kill Statistics

Type Aircraft	Destroyed	Probables	Damaged
MiG-15	490	86	502
Tu-2	9	0	2
Il-12	1	0	0
La-9	6	0	1
La-11	2	0	0
Totals:	**508**	**86**	**505**

By Squadron

334th FS – 143.5 kills, 28 probables, 149 damaged   **336th FS** – 112.5 kills, 19 probables, 119 damaged

335th FS – 223.5 kills, 24 probables, 156 damaged   **4th FW** – 28.5 kills, 15 probables, 81 damaged
(kills made by pilots assigned to the Group or Wing HQ)

By Month

1950		**1951**		**1952**		**1953**	
December	– 7	January	– 0	January	– 5	January	– 14
		February	– 0	February	– 7	February	– 39
		March	– 1	March	– 24	March	– 21
		April	– 14	April	– 20	April	– 8
		May	– 5	May	– 23	May	– 32
		June	– 10	June	– 15	June	– 44
		July	– 6	July	– 8	July	– 21
		August	– 4	August	– 21		
		September	– 12	September	– 36		
		October	– 24	October	– 14		
		November	– 25	November	– 9	**Total**	**– 508**
		December	– 22	December	– 17		

4th FW F-86 Sabre Losses in Korea/FEAF

These totals include losses from MiG-15s, AAA, fuel starvation, pilot error and anything considered operational

1950		**1951**		**1952**		**1953**	
December	– 2	January	– 0	January	– 4	January	– 2
		February	– 2	February	– 6	February	– 3
		March	– 0	March	– 4	March	– 3
		April	– 3	April	– 2	April	– 3
		May	– 4	May	– 8	May	– 4
		June	– 5	June	– 3	June	– 3
		July	– 3	July	– 6	July	– 5
		August	– 2	August	– 4		
		September	– 6	September	– 9		
		October	– 7	October	– 6		
		November	– 4	November	– 3		
		December	– 8	December	– 1		

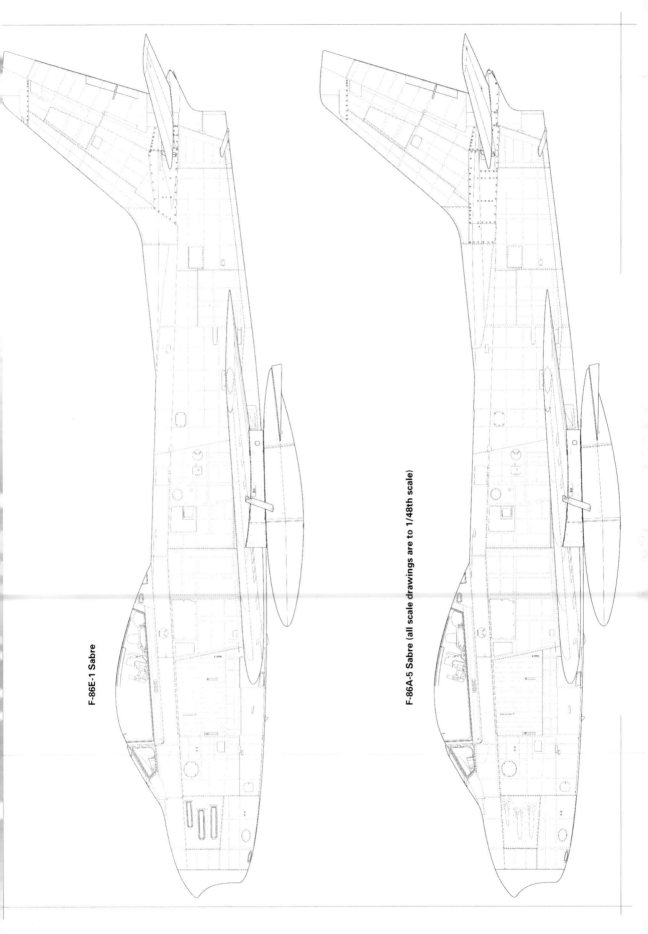

F-86E-1 Sabre

F-86A-5 Sabre (all scale drawings are to 1/48th scale)

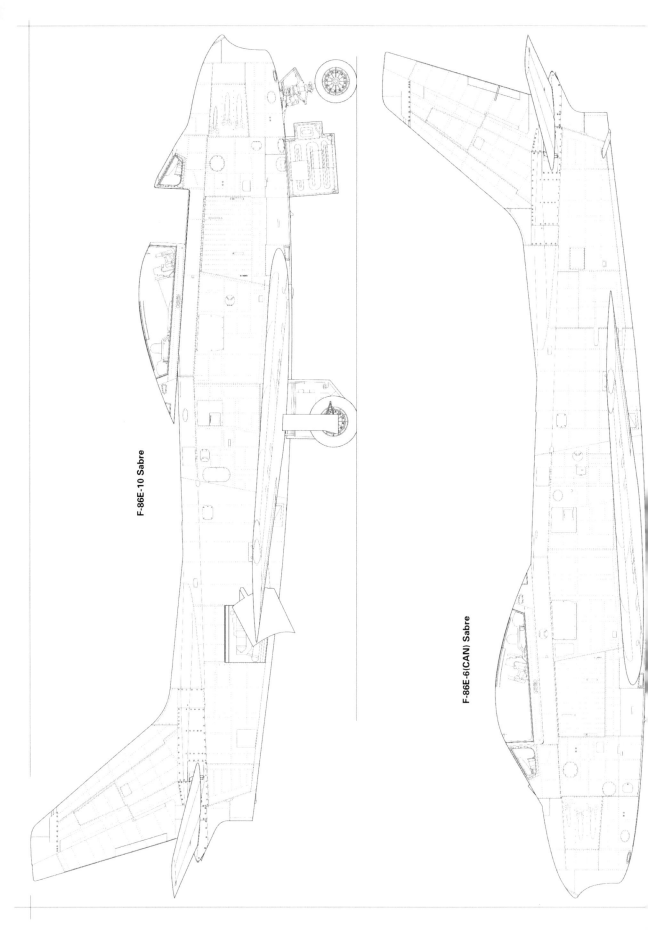

F-86E-10 Sabre

F-86E-6(CAN) Sabre

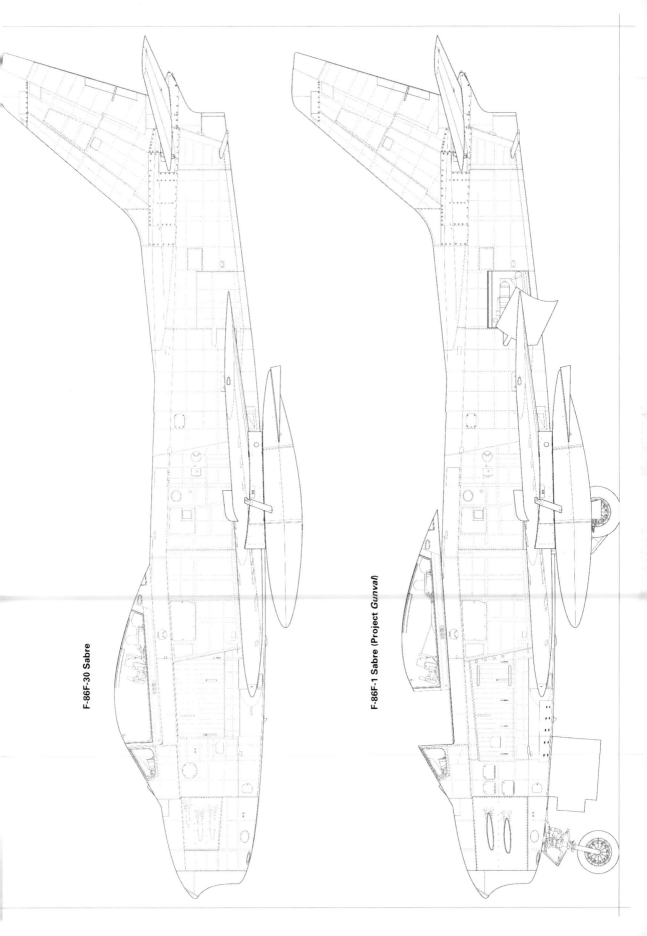

F-86F-30 Sabre

F-86F-1 Sabre (Project *Gunval*)

1

F-86A-5 48-297 *Margie* of the 334th FS, Kimpo AB, December 1950

This aircraft was amongst the initial batch of Sabres sent to the FEAF with the 4th FW in late 1950. The wing's 'Dash-5' F-86s were some of the earliest production models to come off the North American production line for the USAF in the summer of 1949. 48-297 was assigned to the 334th FS throughout its short combat career, and the jet was eventually written off on 11 July 1951 when its pilot could not recover from a spin during a training flight from Johnson AB.

2

F-86A-5 49-1089 *Punkin'-Head* of Capt Morris Pitts, 336th FS, Kimpo AB, December 1950

49-1089 was also an early-production jet that accompanied the 4th FW to Japan, this aircraft being one of the 336th FS machines that made the trip as deck cargo aboard a fast civilian-registered oiler. Assigned to Capt Morris Pitts, the Sabre was written off when experimental high explosive 0.50-cal ammunition blew up in the jet's right gun bay whilst the fighter was on a patrol on 10 May 1951. The explosion severed numerous hydraulic lines in the aircraft, resulting in the undercarriage collapsing when pilot 1Lt Ward Hitt attempted to land at Taegu AB.

3

F-86A-5 49-1109 of Capt Ralph D Gibson, 335th FS, Suwon AB, September 1951

Gibson became the USAF's third jet ace while flying missions in this Sabre between May and September 1951. The jet had no known names or artwork applied to it whilst assigned to him. The fighter was also used by fellow ace 1Lt Richard Becker to claim his first two MiG-15 kills (on 22 April and 8 July 1951) and a damaged (also on 8 July). Shortly after Gibson completed his tour, 49-1109 was shot down by a MiG-15 on 24 October 1951, its pilot being made a PoW.

4

F-86A-5 49-1175 *PEG O' MY HEART* of 1Lt Joseph E Fields, 336th FS, Kimpo AB, September 1952

Bearing a 336th FS 'Rocketeers' badge on its starboard side, along with 1Lt Fields' *PEG O' MY HEART* titling (the port side of the aircraft bore the legend *Paul's MiG Killer*), 49-1175 was one of the last F-86A-5s assigned to the 4th FW. 1Lt Fields was credited with 1.5 MiG kills while flying this Sabre, which survived the war and was eventually passed on to the Oregon ANG's 123rd FS in April 1954.

5

F-86A-5 49-1184 *Miss Behaving* of Capt Richard Becker, 334th FS, Suwon AB, Spring 1951

Part of the second batch of 'Dash-5s' to come off the production line, this aircraft had an interesting combat career with the 4th FW. Although assigned to ace Capt Richard Becker, he failed to achieve a single claim in the fighter. However, World War 2 ace, and future Sabre ace (with the 51st FW), Maj William Whisner claimed a MiG-15 kill and one

damaged in this Sabre on 8 November 1951 during his brief spell with the 334th FS. It was also assigned to Capt Don Torres of the 336th FS. USAF records show that the jet was damaged in combat with MiG-15s over the Han River on 4 December 1951, forcing the pilot to eject.

6

F-86A-5 49-1217 of 1Lt James Leatherbee, 334th FS, Suwon AB, Spring 1951

Another early A-model to see combat with the 4th FW in 1950-51, this aircraft features the wing's trademark black and white fuselage bands which decorated all Sabres in-theatre until the autumn of 1951. 49-1217 was assigned to 1Lt James Leatherbee, who often flew missions as wingman for aces Capts James Jabara and Richard Becker in the early months of 1951. This particular aircraft survived its long spell in combat and was eventually issued to the California ANG's 196th FS at Ontario International Airport in March 1954. Somehow, the veteran jet was not scrapped following its retirement, and the Sabre is presently in storage in California following many years as an exhibit in the Planes of Fame Museum at Chino Airport, on the outskirts of Los Angeles.

7

F-86E-1 50-623 *Pretty Mary and The J's* of Col Harrison Thyng (4th FW CO), Kimpo AB, May 1952

Flown by World War 2 Spitfire ace, and wing CO, Col Harrison Thyng, this aircraft was maintained by the 335th FS – Thyng would usually fly with this squadron when patrolling 'MiG Alley'. One of the first E-models to reach the 4th FW (it was initially assigned to the 336th FS), 50-623 was used by future 51st FW ace 1Lt Robert Moore to claim his first kill on 28 October 1951 while still serving with the 336th FS. The final fate of this machine remains unknown.

8

F-86E-1 50-625 *MR. BONES "V"* of Maj Winton Marshall (335th FS CO), Kimpo AB, December 1951

Maj Winton 'Bones' Marshall was assigned this new E-1 towards the end of his spell as CO of the 335th FS, his command lasting from late June 1951 through to January 1952. One of the wing's first E-models, the jet is adorned with 13 stars which denote his 6.5 kills and 6 damaged claims. Marshall was credited with a mixed bag of victories, as he destroyed 4.5 MiGs, a Tu-2 and a rare La-9 – he claimed the latter two to 'make ace' on 30 November 1951. This aircraft was subsequently passed on to Capt James Horowitz of the 335th FS's crack 'D Flight' in 1952, and it survived the war to be assigned to the 35th FW in November 1953 following the 4th FW's return to the USA.

9

F-86E-5 50-648 *Pretty Mary/EIGHT BALL EXPRESS* of Capt Clay O Keen, 336th FS, Kimpo AB, 1952

This aircraft spent time with both the 334th and 336th FS during its long frontline tour, being assigned to several different pilots and flown by many more. During 1952 the Sabre was mostly used by Capt Clay O Keen, who had the fighter's distinctive nickname painted on its fuselage. This was Keen's second conflict, as he had also seen combat flying P-38s in Burma during World War 2. 50-648 survived the war and was eventually transferred to the 35th FW in Japan in June 1954.

10

F-86E-10 51-2722 *VIRGINIA BELLE/GOPHER PATROL* of Maj William K Thomas, 335th FS, Kimpo AB, June 1952

Only the fifth 'Dash-10' to roll off the North American production line, this jet was delivered to the 4th FW in October 1951. The Sabre's assigned pilot was Maj William K Thomas, who was responsible for naming it. He also claimed a single MiG-15 kill with the jet on 31 May 1952. Aside from the red star, the Sabre also boasted two red locomotive silhouettes, denoting successful strafing attacks on trains in North Korea. At the end of Thomas's tour 51-2722 was passed on to 1Lt Ira Porter, who claimed two MiG-15s with it on 4 September 1952. Suffering a flame-out while attacking the second communist fighter, Porter was forced to land on mud flats south of Antung, from where he was quickly rescued by helicopter.

11

F-86E-10 51-2747 *Stud/HONEST JOHN* of Col Walker Mahurin (4th FG Deputy CO), Kimpo AB, December 1951

One of the 4th FW's most photographed Sabres, this aircraft was assigned to the 336th FS and flown by World War 2 ace Col Walker 'Bud' Mahurin whilst both Deputy CO and CO of the 4th FG. A pioneer in the use of the Sabre as a close air support fighter-bomber, Mahurin was shot down (in F-86E-10 51-2789) by AAA during just such an attack on 13 May 1952, and spent the rest of the war as a PoW. 51-2747 survived the war, however, and was subsequently posted to the 35th FW.

12

F-86E-10 51-2767 *THE CHOPPER* of Maj Felix Asla (336th FS CO), Kimpo AB, July 1952

Killed in action in this very aircraft, Asla had four victories and five damaged to his credit at the time of his demise on 1 August 1952. He was shot down over North Korea by a MiG-15 that he mistakenly thought was his wingman joining up with him from the rear. The first of Asla's victories had been scored in February 1952 whilst he was serving with the 334th FS.

13

F-86E-10 51-2791 *Dupe's Delight/Jaline* of 1Lt Forist G Dupree, 336th FS, Kimpo AB, May 1953

This aircraft was used by 1Lt Dupree to claim a single MiG-15 kill 16 May 1953 – he was one of eight 4th FW pilots to score victories on this date. The fighter was named in honour of the pilot's wife, Jaline. Later seeing action with the 51st FW's 25th FS at Suwon, this aircraft survived the war and was also passed on to the 35th FW at Johnson AB.

14

F-86E-10 51-2794 *NEWARK FIRE BALL* of Capt Karl Dittmer, 335th FS, Kimpo AB, August 1952

Initially assigned to 1Lt Henry A Crescibene, who was credited with a MiG-15 kill in it on 4 August 1952, 51-2794

was subsequently passed on to Capt Karl Dittmer. The latter, who hailed from Newark, New Jersey, claimed two MiG kills on 9 October 1952. This Sabre survived combat tours with both the 335th and the 334th FSs, after which it was assigned to the 35th FW post-war.

15

F-86E-10 51-2794 *Gweny* of Capt Maynard Stogdill, 334th FS, Kimpo AB, March 1953

This was how 51-2794 appeared whilst assigned to Capt Maynard Stogdill of the 334th FS, who had the name *Gweny* applied to both sides of the fighter's nose. He used it to claim his sole MiG-15 kill on 29 March 1953.

16

F-86E-10 51-2800 *Liza Gal/El Diablo* of Capt Chuck Owens, 336th FS, Kimpo AB, February 1952

This aircraft bore elaborate artwork and victory symbols that featured red stars and truck and tank silhouettes, with the latter revealing that the pilot was particularly fond of ground strafing. The eight stars below the cockpit must have denoted kills credited to other pilots in 51-2800, for Capt Owens did not claim his first officially recognised victory until two-and-a-half months after the aircraft had been written off on 13 February 1952.

17

F-86E-10 51-2834 *JOLLEY ROGER* of Capt Clifford Jolley, 335th FS, Kimpo AB, October 1952

This profile depicts 51-2834 in early October 1952, just days prior to Capt Jolley claiming his seventh, and last, kill in it on the 11th of that month. Declared tour-expired shortly after this, Jolley returned home and his Sabre was transferred to the 336th FS, where it remained until war's end.

18

F-86E-10 51-2834 *Joanne*, 336th FS, Kimpo AB, Spring 1953

51-2834 was given the name *Joanne* soon after its transfer to the 336th FS. The latter unit's distinctive 'Rocketeers' emblem was also applied to the fighter in place of the 335th FS's Indian Chief. The nine kill symbols that adorned the right side of the fuselage included seven credited to Jolley. Like most E-models still serving with the 4th FW when the ceasefire came into effect, this aircraft was passed on to the 35th FW in Japan.

19

F-86F-1 51-2857 of Capt Manuel J Fernandez, 334th FS, Kimpo AB, May 1953

Although flown by the third ranking Sabre ace of the war, this aircraft was bereft of any specific name or nose art. Fernandez flew a number of different F-86s during his 125-mission tour, but most of his early kills were claimed in F-86E-10 51-2830 and his final half-dozen in 51-2857. This aircraft also proved popular with the 334th FS's other leading ace, Maj James Jabara, who scored several victories with it after Fernandez had been ordered home. Later transferred to the 336th FS in the last weeks of the war, the aircraft subsequently saw post-war service with the 8th FBG from Itazuke AB, Japan.

20

F-86F-2 51-12867 *Gunval* of Lt Col George Jones, 335th FS, Kimpo AB, January 1953

Specially adapted to carry four 20 mm cannon instead of the standard six 0.50-cal machine guns as part of Project *Gunval*, this aircraft was the personal mount of project leader Lt Col George Jones. Having claimed kills with the 4th and 51st FWs in 1951-52, Jones 'made ace' in this aircraft on 29 March 1953. The jet returned the USA in May 1953 and was taken on strength by the 3595th Training Wing at Nellis AFB.

21

F-86F-10 51-12941 of Col James Johnson (4th FW CO), Kimpo AB, July 1953

This was one of the few Sabres to boast a kill tally scored by a single pilot, namely Col James Johnson. Devoid of nose art, the jet was assigned to Johnson in early 1953, soon after he had 'made ace'. CO of the 4th FW from 11 November 1952 through to 9 August 1953, Col Johnson led the wing when it was running up its biggest scores – he usually flew missions with the 335th FS. Johnson's victories were claimed between 13 January and 30 June 1953. 51-12941 was one of 320 F-86Fs passed on to the Chinese Nationalist Air Force in late 1954.

22

F-86F-10 51-12953 of Maj Vermont Garrison (335th FS CO), Kimpo AB, June 1953

Maj Garrison used this F-86F-10 for most of his later kills, including his tenth, and last, on 19 July 1953. Many of his earlier victories had been achieved in F-86F-10 51-12959. Yet another late war Sabre devoid of artwork bar the unit badge, 51-12953 was also supplied to the Chinese Nationalist Air Force in 1954.

23

F-86F-15 51-12976 *Speedy Cec* of 2Lt Cecil Lefevers, 336th FS, Kimpo AB, June 1953

Although only issued to the 4th FW in June 1953, this aircraft remained in Korea with the wing well into 1954. It was initially assigned to 2Lt Cecil Lefevers, who used it to claim a share in a MiG-15 downed with Capt George W Love on 30 June. Lefevers extended his tour after the ceasefire and flew numerous escort and reconnaissance missions in this jet along the North Korean coast. Soon after Lefevers finished his tour, 51-12976 was reassigned to the 335th FS.

24

F-86F-15 51-12976 *Chopper* of 1Lt Harry T Hagaman, 335th FS, Kimpo AB, late 1953

Once transferred to the 335th, *Speedy Cec* soon became 1Lt Hagaman's *Chopper*. A Marine Corps exchange pilot, Hagaman also had the fighter's fuselage adorned with a large USMC emblem. In 1954, he and the jet rotated back and forth between Kimpo AB and Itazuke AB, in Japan. Surviving its tenure with the 4th FW, 51-12976 was passed on to the Chinese Nationalist Air Force in late 1954.

25

F-86E-6(CAN) 52-2856 *BETTY BOOTS* of Capt Karl Dittmer, 335th FS, Kimpo AB, October 1952

One of a small number of Canadair-built Sabres to see combat in Korea, this aircraft arrived at Kimpo in late September 1952. The jet was immediately assigned to Capt Karl Dittmer, who was one of the 4th FW's most talented artists. Indeed, his work adorned a number of 335th FS Sabres during this period. Dittmer was also no slouch as a pilot either, having claimed a single kill in World War 2 flying P-51Ds. He subsequently scored three MiG-15 victories in 1952, including two in one day in this jet on 9 October. 52-2856 was passed on to the 336th FS in 1953, and it survived the conflict to be handed over to the Chinese Nationalist Air Force the following year.

26

F-86F-30 52-4341 *"MIG POISON"* of Maj James Hagerstrom, 67th FBS/18th FBG, Osan AB, May 1953

This aircraft belongs to the sole Sabre pilot to 'make ace' with the 18th FBG, namely 67th FBS CO Maj James Hagerstrom. A Pacific War P-40 Warhawk ace from 1943-44, Hagerstrom gained Sabre ace status on 27 March 1953. He qualifies for inclusion in this volume because his first two kills in Korea were scored with the 334th and 335th FSs in November and December 1952. Reluctantly transferred to the newly re-equipped 18th FBG in January 1953, Hagerstrom flew 'Dash-30' fighter-bombers for the next sixth months. He claimed a further 6.5 MiG-15 kills with the 67th FBS between 25 February and 16 May 1953.

27

F-86F-30 52-4468 *Lorrie* of 1Lt Richard Keener, 335th FS, Kimpo AB, July 1953

Issued to 1Lt Keener right at the end of the war, this jet flew only a handful of missions before the ceasefire came into effect at midnight on 27 July 1953. Keener had spent the final two months of the conflict flying as a wingman for some of the high-scoring 335th FS aces, logging 40 combat missions before the war ended. He remained with the wing until the end of the year, flying many post-war patrols from Kimpo AB. This F-86 was eventually passed on to the 58th FBW, which became the final USAF Sabre outfit in Korea in 1955.

28

F-86F-30 52-4513 of Maj James Jabara, 334th FS, Kimpo AB, July 1953

Like many of the 4th FW's high-scoring aces, the wing's ranking ace, Maj Jabara, did not personalise his jets other than to have his victory stars applied to them. 52-4513 was the final F-86 flown in combat by Jabara, and as such it boasts 22 victory symbols, denoting not only his 15 kills but also his three probables and four of his six damaged claims. Like most F-86Fs that survived the conflict, this aircraft was supplied to the Chinese Nationalist Air Force in 1954.

29

F-86F-30 52-4541 *Patty II/DIMPS V* of the 336th FS, Kimpo AB, June 1953

Amongst the last batch of F-models sent to the 4th FW prior to the ceasefire, this aircraft was flown by several pilots during the summer of 1953. Its entire combat tour was spent with the 336th FS, after which the jet was eventually transferred (in early 1955) to the 58th FBW at Osan AB, in South Korea.

30

**F-86F-30 52-4545 *SALLY ANN/SCREAMIN' EAGLE* of
1Lt Dusty Showen, 334th FS, Kimpo AB, July 1953**

Arriving in Korea at around the same time as the Sabre
featured in the previous profile, this aircraft was marked with
a retro-style unit badge on its fuselage. The Sabre's assigned
pilot, 1Lt 'Dusty' Showen, flew 36 combat missions in the jet
prior to the end of the war.

31

**F-86F-30 52-4589 *JACKIE'S BOY* of 1Lt Edwin Scarff,
334th FS, Kimpo AB, July 1953**

Yet another late-delivery 'Dash-30' featuring the retro insignia,
52-4589 was amongst the last F-models to be issued to the
4th FW during the final weeks of the war. These newer
Sabres saw extensive post-war service monitoring the
ceasefire both from bases in South Korea and Japan. And like
most 'Dash-30s', this aircraft found its way into the ranks of
the Chinese Nationalist Air Force in 1954.

32

**F-86F-30 52-4773 *Mississippi Gambler/Arkansas Traveler*
of 1Lt John Tabor, 335th FS, Kimpo AB, June 1953**

1Lt Tabor completed 54 missions in this aircraft, which he
also named after his native Mississippi. Credited with two
MiG-15 probables and one damaged in the early summer of
1953, Tabor remained with the 335th in Korea for the first few
months of peace until he was tour-expired.

33

**F-86F-30 52-4773 *Mississippi Gambler/Arkansas Traveler*
of 1Lt John Tabor, 335th FS, Kimpo AB, June 1953**

Tabor's Sabre carried the name *ARKANSAS TRAVELER* on its
right side, this sobriquet being chosen by its crew chief
Airman 2C Verlon George. The names carried on the right
side of most F-86s in Korea had been chosen by their
dedicated groundcrew. Like most 4th FW F-86Fs that survived the war, this aircraft was transferred to the Chinese
Nationalist Air Force in 1954.

BIBLIOGRAPHY

Frederick C 'Boots' Blesse, *'Check Six'*. Champlin Fighter Museum Press, 1987

Davis, Larry, *North American F-86 Sabre – Wings of Fame volume 10*. Aerospace Publishing, 1998

Dorr, Robert F, Lake, Jon and Thompson, Warren, *Osprey Aircraft of the Aces 4 – Korean War Aces*. Osprey Publishing, 1995

Futrell, Robert F, *The United States Air Force in Korea 1950-1953*

Henderson, John, *Personal Historical Papers on 4th Wing,1950-1951*

McLaren, David, *F-86 Losses in FEAF (December 1950-July 1953)*

Olynyk, Frank, *Stars & Bars*. Grub Street, 1995

Ravenstein, Charles A, *Air Force Combat Wings (1947-1977)*. Office of Air Force History, 1984

Spurr, Russell, *Enter the Dragon*. Newmarket Press, 1988

Thompson, Warren E and MacLaren, David R, *MiG Alley*. Specialty Press, 2002

Wagner, Ray, *The North American Sabre*. Doubleday Publishing, 1963

Walter, Lon, *Sabre*, Jet Classics, Summer 1996

Air Force Historical Research Center, *Korean War Victory Credits*

Air Force Magazine, September 1958

INDEX

References to illustrations are shown in **bold**.
Plates are shown with page and caption locators in brackets.